My First
True Love

COLLECTED STORIES

by
Nina Lee Colwill

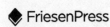

One Printers Way
Altona, MB R0G 0B0
Canada

www.friesenpress.com

Copyright © 2024 by Nina Lee Colwill
First Edition — 2024

Foreword by W.D. Valgardson
Illustrations by Katrina Anderson and Guy Anderson
Photograph by Barbara Czarniawska

Contributors to *My First True Love* have permission to re-submit their stories to other publications.

All rights reserved.

No part of this publication may be reproduced in any form, or by any means, electronic or mechanical, including photocopying, recording, or any information browsing, storage, or retrieval system, without permission in writing from FriesenPress.

ISBN
978-1-03-919541-7 (Hardcover)
978-1-03-919540-0 (Paperback)
978-1-03-919542-4 (eBook)

1. FAMILY & RELATIONSHIPS, LOVE & ROMANCE

Distributed to the trade by The Ingram Book Company

**Other Books
by Nina Lee Colwill**

The Psychology of Sex Differences (with Hilary Lips)

The New Partnership: Women and Men in Organizations

The Essence of Women in Management (with Susan Vinnicombe)
(Polish edition: *Kobieta w Zarządzaniu*, translation by Domański Piotr)

Table of Contents

Foreword	xi
Preface	xiii
My First True Loves: An Introduction	1
Children's Loves	7
Maureen Arnason – Head Over Heels at Seven	8
Carol Dahlstrom – The Most Handsome of Dentists	10
Gunnar Wahlström – Floating Away with Hillivi	12
Carl Pauptit – Falling in Love at Church Camp	13
Linda Grijalva – Kissing and Telling	15
Bev Cameron – First Kindred Spirit	17
Marie Graham – True Love, First Kiss	18
Jack Hauen – Dance Club	21
Diane Cooley – Last Week I Told My Husband About My Secret Love	21
Daniel Perlman – Preschool Polygamy: My First Love Affair	23
Barbara Czarniawska – The Red Bag: A Love Story	26
Bjørn Erik Ramtvedt – A Healing Love at Five	28
Teenage Loves	31
Audrey Ingólfsdóttir – When Love Isn't Enough	32
Kelly Arndt – #4	35
Sylvia Anderson Koshyk – The Circuitous Route	37
Irene Way – Forbidden Love	41

Les Rankin – Runaway Love   46
Hervé Corvellec – Things Forgotten, One Remembers   46

Loves That Lasted   49
Hazel Colwill – The Best Christmas Gift Ever   50
Fred Starke – The First Week of December   55
Lynn Lakusiak – The Look   57
Alice Hogue – The Dance   59
Shirley Younkin – Close Encounters of the Noisy Kind   61
Nan Hayman – Chance Encounters   62
Jón Bjarman – Falling in Love with an Angel   63
Kristín Aðalsteinsdóttir – Him   65
Hallgrímur Indriðason – Her   67
Brent Patterson – Love at First Sight   68
Marie-Josée Paquet – Babe: What's in a Name?   70

Lost Loves   73
A Storyteller From Palermo – A Lost Hand   74
Gwen Kalansky – Thank You, Nick   75
Geraldine Gilmour – Never Forgotten   78
Conni Cartlidge – Percentages   82
Wynne – None Could Compare   86
Jay Williams – What's Love Got to Do With the BuRec?   89
Larry Denchuk – Grandma's House   91

Not All Love Is Romantic   99
Rachel – My Mother and Me   100
Denise Ommanney – An Early Grace   101
Heather Drozd – Love at First Sight   103
Angela Anderson – Blooming Amidst the Rocks   105

Sondra Mackenzie-Plovie – How My Father's Love
    Shaped Me   110
Verna Korkie – Riches to Rags to Riches   113
Elaine Rounds – Grandma Kate   121
W. D. (Bill) Valgardson – Innocence   126
Joanne Klassen – Uncle Willie and Me   131
Ainsley A. Thorarinson S. Bloomer – Thank You, Great-Uncle
    Carl Hansson   134
Sodhi Pillay – Benny's Bunch   137
Shirley Younkin – The Wonderful Power of the
    Written Word   143
Tanya Speight – Love in the Therapy Room   144

For the Love of Cuddling   149

Jamie Koshyk – My Lovely, Snappy, Snarly Snoopy   150
Tiffany Berman – Pure Comfort   151
Vivian Anderson – Love at First Sight   154
Maureen Morrish – The Gift of Heartbreak   156
Carol (Reeves) Pauptit – A Treasured Possession   159
Fred Anderson – Loving to Death   160
Zen Sigmundson – Struby: The Cat in the Basement   162
Guy Anderson – My Hamster   163

Love Knows No Bounds   167

Blanche Clow – My Skates: Loved, Loved, Loved My Skates   168
Christine Smith – Jumping, Spinning, Gliding   169
Karen Minden – Clear, Crisp Love   172
Ulla Eriksson-Zetterquist – Truly, Truly Loving Reading   173
Stefan Arora-Jonsson – A Summer Romance   175
Deborah Schnitzer – cigarettes   177

Valerie Parker Mackenzie – Comfort, Trust, Security ... 182
Randell Parker – The Power and the Heat of First Love ... 183
Christina Garsten – Stepping into the World ... 184
Michelle Kube – The Music Took My Hand: A Love Story ... 185
Graham MacLennan – Italian Food is Romance ... 188
Anonymous – The Minnesota–Norwegian Fisherman's Anthem ... 190
Jason Thompson – The King ... 191
Lorraine Sproxton – Romancing the Lake ... 194
Marjorie Anderson – Sojo on My Mind ... 197
Gayleen Hutchings – My Favourite Dress ... 200
Ann MacDonald – Oh-h-h-h-h Canada!! ... 201
Katrina Anderson (aka Fontana Swing) – Dear Piano, I Love You ... 203

And Where Can Love Be Found? ... **207**
Liane Faulder – My Own. My Jane. ... 207
Emily A. Bryant – The Many Faces of Love ... 210
Lilly Julia Schubert Walker-Kittsley – The Search for True Love ... 213

Acknowledgements ... **217**

To Colton, Kyle, Vala, and Ari,
grandchildren extraordinaire,
who taught me about a different kind of love.

Foreword

Nowadays it's a sign of integrity to admit to a conflict of interest before recommending something.

So, I'll fess up right now. In fact, I have two confessions. First, I have a piece about my first love included in this book. And second, the compiler, Nina, and I decided we'd be brother and sister when she was sixteen and I was twenty-one. My parents never gave me a sister. Her parents never gave her a brother. Sometimes you just have to create what you want.

Yet biases aside, I truly believe that this is a significant book because it stands against all the heartbreak I see in the media: gossip, despair, divorces, and deaths. The news media thrive on tragedies large and small. It's easy to have the experience of love washed away in the maelstrom of Hollywood divorces, accounts of physical violence, endless gossip, and daily sexploitation. This book is a reminder to all of us of what our first loves were like, how intense they were, how much they mattered, and how, even today, they are part of who we are.

In writing my story and reading the others, I realized that I could have written about a number of first loves. I could have written about the girl next door. I think she was three and I was four. I used to sit on her front steps and wait for her to come out to play. I even made, or tried to make, a necklace from dandelions for her. Or I could have written about my first dog. He was a consolation gift after my brother was born, and I was no longer king of the castle. My grandmother, however, was the centre of my universe and my first true love.

When we are young, we bestow our love on people, pets, and objects. For one person in this book, a first love was the family dentist, for another it was a hamster, and for a third it was a fishing lure.

When we love, we take on risk. As the years pass, we take that risk many times. Often our love is not returned or, if returned, is later denied. There's a whole industry based on that plot—novels, plays, movies, TV shows. After we've been disappointed a number of times, we learn to be more cautious, to tell ourselves and others not to be so trusting, not to be so naïve. Be wary. Test the water.

What I like about *My First True Love* is that it deals with the beginning, before all our guards are up, before we've become cynical.

I believe that that is important. We need to be reminded of our innate capacity to love. We need to be reminded how natural it is to love something or someone. If we lose that, it's important that we find it again, perhaps this time with more careful vetting, without so much of the innocence that makes us vulnerable.

One of the greatest compliments I ever received was from a six-year-old neighbour. She confided in one of my cousins, who was her best friend, "When I grow up, I'm going to marry someone just like Billy." I think I was around thirty-five at the time. That is a treasure to hold in my heart forever.

I've delighted in all these stories. I find them heartwarming. A best thing about them is their honesty. Another best thing is their reminder of what we are capable of, what we have offered with our hearts, and what we can offer again. It's a reminder of our earlier selves. I hope these stories will cause the readers to remember and treasure those earlier selves.

W. D. Valgardson,
Victoria, BC

Preface

> Indeed, Past is never buried –
> It breathes silently,
> Deep inside,
> Distant yet alive.
>
> - Debatrayee Banerjee

The idea for this book emerged one cold winter's day as I drove across the Manitoba prairie to visit the parents of my first true love. Somewhere between Brandon and Gimli, I began to marvel at the bond that returned me to Dale's family decades after we had married other people and I had immersed myself in my husband, Dennis's, large, loving family. (Dennis and I have ten siblings and some hundred first cousins between us.) And as I drove, I began to wonder, "Were all first loves as significant as mine has proven to be?"

I mulled over that question for several years and finally decided to ask it of other people. I started with friends and relatives, and from their stories I learned that for them, too, first love can have a lasting impact. I was amazed at the detail and depth of emotion their memories generated, decades after the writers' first loves were no longer in their lives.

Compiling this book has been pure joy for me—because of the wonderful stories I've gathered, of course, but also because of a sense of freedom from the rigours of science that I never experienced in the years I spent as a professor and a researcher in psychology and business. The people who contributed to this book weren't part of a scientific study. They weren't chosen through random sampling. They were contacted by e-mail, cornered at parties, or recommended by others. They were my friends, relatives, and colleagues and, through word of mouth, their friends, relatives, and colleagues.

No rules applied here. Story length varied widely. More women than men wrote for this book because more women than men were suggested as potential storytellers, and more men than women said, "No, thanks." (Or sometimes just "No.") Most of the Europeans whose stories are captured here are academics because most of the Europeans I know are in academia. The North American storytellers cover a broad range of occupations and lifestyles.

It has been my great privilege to work on *My First True Love*—to open a window into the love lives of other people. I laughed out loud at some of these stories and sobbed my way through others. Before I was able to read to a gathering of my cousins the story that my Aunt Hazel Colwill had written at age ninety-eight, I re-read it aloud to myself ten times so I could get through it without tears.

Several of these stories began when the storytellers were preschoolers. Dan Perlman was four when he became involved in a love triangle with Pixie and Jeannie, and Bjørn Erik Ramtvedt's first love transformed him from a shy child into a brave and confident five-year-old.

It's not surprising that some of the storytellers fell in love for the first time as teenagers. It was with her teenage love, in fact, that Audrey Ingólfsdóttir learned that love is not always enough. A few of the teenage romances in this book lasted a lifetime; others were cut short, sometimes by mutual agreement, sometimes regrettably.

We can love people, it turns out, that we don't even know. Kelly Arndt tells of her intense and long-lasting love for #4, a hockey player she met only three times, and then only long enough to say a hesitant "Hello."

But not all love is romantic. In compiling this book, I learned a great deal about the breadth of love from writers like Joanne Klassen, whose childhood memory of Uncle Willie still brings a smile to her face; like Sondra Mackenzie-Plovie, whose love for her father taught her the qualities she required in a life partner; and like Shirley Younkin, whose Grade 2 teacher so affected her life that she still has the letter Miss White wrote to her in 1953.

Some of these stories are about cuddly nonhumans. Tiffany Berman describes her childhood love for the little cat that eased her passage into life in a new country. And Jamie Koshyk relates the tale of Snoopy, the dog that only she could love.

Not all the stories in this book are about living things, human or animal. Christine Smith and Blanche Clow, two women who grew up in different countries, truly loved their first white figure skates. Their stories aren't merely about the joy of a material possession; they're also about the freedom they experienced sailing across the ice into new and different worlds.

As I worked on this book, I continued to relearn the same lesson: First true love never dies. Yet having lost that love, we can go on to love again. And again. Irene Way fell in love with a boy whose "goodness, tolerance, and patience" captured her heart. She lost him to the Church and fell in love again—with the man who became her husband and the father of their eight children. Lilly Walker-Kittsley loved her devoted husband completely and undeniably, lost him to cancer, and loved completely and undeniably once again.

I've given you but a sprinkling of the wide variety of stories in this book, trying to choose examples that weren't spoilers for the full story. The seventy-eight contributors provided me with generous glimpses into their lives that moved me far more than I could ever have expected. Humorous, tender, or sad, the stories entrusted to me and now entrusted to you are all poignant. And they ring true. Time may have altered specific details, but their essence, their core, bears the stamp of truth.

My First True Loves:
An Introduction

> We are shaped and fashioned by those we love.
>
> - Debatrayee Banerjee

Dale and I were students at Gimli Collegiate when we fell in love. I was sixteen and he was seventeen. I had dated several boys and gone steady with three, but Dale was my first true love.

Dale was tall and gangly, with a sweet, boyish face that announced his gentle nature. I can see him still, wearing runners and an old brown suede bomber jacket at thirty below zero, earmuffs on his ears and hands in his pockets. He had a shy, crooked smile and a lock of blond hair that was continually falling over his forehead. We fell in love as only teenagers can fall in love—as if no one and nothing else in the world mattered, as if no one and nothing could intervene.

Then life intervened. A year after Dale and I started dating, my father was transferred from Gimli to Toronto. And as we drove the 2,000 kilometres to our new home, I was sure I would die of a broken heart. I would never love anyone else again. I would get a job in Toronto and save my money and move back to Gimli.

But it didn't take me long to become immersed in a social whirl of new boyfriends, and it wasn't long before Dale found his new and lasting true love—the woman he was to marry.

Two years passed, and I did come back to Gimli. I stayed with friends, revisited my favourite haunts, and caught up with my old high-school buddies, some of whom were married by then. Dale and I decided to get together for a visit, and I wondered how it would feel to see him again. But as we updated each other on our lives, it became clear that time and other people had changed us. Although my seventeen-year-old self would never have believed it, my nineteen-year-old self could see that we had made the transition from sweethearts to friends.

And then, a few days later, a young man came to Gimli to see his cousins—the very friends I was visiting. That's when I came face to face with Dennis Anderson—my new and lasting true love, the man I was to marry.

* * *

The story of my first true love is just the beginning of a much longer story—a story about the profound effect that first love can have on the rest of a person's life, the effect that my first true love has had on the rest of my life. Falling in love with Dale led me into a relationship with his

My First True Loves: An Introduction

family—a family bond that is as real to me as if I'd been born into it or married into it.

Yes, my first true love has touched me in ways I could never have predicted. Dale died in a tragic accident when he was thirty, long after we had gone our separate ways, married, and had two children each. Yet my connection to Dale's family has remained strong. I had grown up in a loving family, and I wasn't searching for more relatives to fill my life. But to my surprise, I found them.

Perhaps my love for Dale readied me to accept more people into my heart. To fall in love with Dale was to love everything about him. And so I fell in love with his parents, Dempsey and Rae, and I fell in love with his brother, Bill.

Bill was one of the "big kids" when I started high school, so I knew him only from afar. We were thrown together when Dale and I started dating, though, and we quickly became fast friends, linked by our love of writing and whatever magical element makes people want to be close to each other. He read my melodramatic poetry and praised a line here, an image there, offering a gentle suggestion: "Maybe try not to evoke God so much."

On New Year's Eve, 1960, when I was sixteen and Bill was twenty-one, three generations of Dale's family gathered for a party in the walk-up apartment in Winnipeg where Bill and his wife, Mary-Anne, lived. As with most sixteen-year-olds, my emotions were close to the surface, and for some reason I fail to remember today, I was feeling particularly sad that evening. Bill noticed and asked me if I wanted to talk. We left the noise of the family party and sat on the steps leading up to his apartment, where he consoled me and brought me out of my teenage angst. Warmed by his wisdom and his caring, I asked him that night if he would be my brother.

Bill had never had a sister and I had never had a brother, a gap in our lives that we eagerly filled for each other. Perhaps we could have bonded more thoroughly had we become blood brother and blood sister, but we both cringed at the idea of cutting into our fingers and drawing blood. As Bill wrote for my book of memories when I turned sixty: "I didn't know it then, but with the wisdom of hindsight, the best day of my life was when Nina asked me to be her brother and I agreed. Being brother and sister can't be easily rent asunder."

And so our siblingship took hold and grew, and six decades later, we're friends with members of each other's extended families. We communicate virtually every day by e-mail and knock on each other's doors whenever we can. We exchange feedback on our writing and give each other birthday parties. We take long walks in Gimli and Victoria, commiserating with each other when things go wrong and rejoicing together when they turn out right. And this year I was thrilled when Billy, as we call him in Gimli, dedicated his latest novel, *In Valhalla's Shadows*, to me.

Bill once introduced me as his sister to a journalist who happened to be interviewing him when I was visiting. She seemed confused and said that she thought he had only one sibling—a brother who had died. "If life doesn't give you what you want," was Bill's response, "you should ask for it."

Bill moved around Canada and USA, and finally ended up at University of Victoria. His parents, Dempsey and Rae, remained in Gimli and became grandparents and great-grandparents. Dennis and I moved around Canada, spent a sabbatical year at Cranfield University in England, and I spent a year at the University of Akureyri in Iceland. And forty-three years after I left for Toronto, I moved back to Gimli with Dennis. I returned to the town that held all the memories of my teenage years, my high-school buddies, and my first true love and his family.

My First True Loves: An Introduction

Then Dempsey died, and Billy asked me to speak at his memorial service. As I prepared my comments, memories of Dempsey came flooding back—memories of that charming man who became my hero, that dapper man in the white shirt, dress pants, and suspenders. I can see him still, leaning against the doorframe of his barbershop, chatting up the passersby, standing by the kitchen stove, waiting for the kettle to boil, pouring water through the filter, pouring me a cup of coffee. But most of all, I can see his face light up whenever we met.

And then Rae died, and Billy asked me to speak at her memorial service as well. Dennis and I had been invited to a wedding in Toronto the weekend of the service, but I dropped Dennis off at the airport and drove back to Gimli to prepare my talk. Again, I was flooded with decades of beautiful memories.

Rae was pretty and smart and fun. She twinkled. She understood. She understood because she listened. Listened deeply.

I remembered how Rae had taught me about feminism without ever saying the word, without ever talking about women's rights. Even in the 1950s, she was paving the way, purely by example, for those of us who were to call ourselves feminists in the 1970s. Rae had what we used to call a man's job. She was manager of the Gimli Credit Union. She *was* the Gimli Credit Union. The credit union safe was kept in her house, and the dining-room table was always covered with papers that we teenagers were never allowed to look at. That certainly impressed us kids.

But what impressed me even more was Rae's physical presence. In the 1950s, when 100-pound girls were wearing skin-tight elastic undergarments to flatten their flat bums and flatten their flat bellies, Rae refused to wear a girdle. She was the only adult woman I knew who didn't wear a girdle. To me she was the freest of free spirits, a woman who considered herself a person first. And simply by living her life, she taught me to believe that I was a person too.

***

As this project unfolded, I began to understand the ways in which love prepared me for love. Being loved by Dale and his family taught me that I was truly loveable—not just to my family, whose love I took for granted, but intrinsically loveable. And knowing myself to be loveable, I could accept nothing less of life than true love.

Perhaps that explains why I can dream a sweet dream about Dale, wake up with a smile, and gaze with love at Dennis sleeping beside me. My first true love made that possible.

Children's Loves

> The events of childhood do not pass but repeat themselves like seasons of the year.
>
> - Eleanor Farjeon

I have a delightful book by Alec Howe and Alison Whyte. Aptly entitled *First Kisses*, it comprises the first-kiss stories of celebrities. And as with many of the stories I collected for this book, I was amazed at the detail of contributions collected decades after the event. Ben Kingsley, for instance, provided a highly specific rendition of his sister's birthday party when he was ten years old and was kissed by every girl in the room: "They all dived on top of me and, squeaking and squealing my name, covered me in kisses, which was wonderful." His sister was not as thrilled as he was, however, and kept hopping about, shouting, "It's my party and these are my guests."

Helen Mirren was completely disenchanted by her first kiss, described as a "squash-your-lips-and-hold-your-breath-as-long-as-possible" event. But Emma Thompson, who experienced her first kiss at age twelve, was so enamoured that she stalked the kisser until "it became so embarrassing he took to hiding behind trees."

The children's love stories you are about to read recall experiences that were much more positive than Helen Mirren's but no less memorable than those of Ben Kingsley and Emma Thompson.

MAUREEN ARNASON

Maureen Arnason is a retired teacher. She lives in Winnipeg but spends much of the year at her cottage in her hometown of Gimli. Although it's not always the wisest course of action, she contends, she has tended to follow the family motto, "If it's worth doing, it's worth doing to excess." She wishes she could apply this belief more often to exercising and less often to drinking wine.

Head Over Heels at Seven

I suppose, when I really think about it, my first love would have been my mother's face, but I can't remember that feeling of love. Hers would have been the first face my weak, little-baby eyes would have recognized as someone who loved me. She would have been the first person that I realized I couldn't live without, literally. But that is not a very thrilling first love.

My first true love was my cousin Dolores's boyfriend, Adriano. He was an Italian pilot training in Gimli back when we still had an airbase.

Children's Loves

I was seven years old, and he was by far the handsomest man I had ever seen. He had dark hair and liquid, brown eyes. I think my little sister, Donna-Lee, loved him, too, though she'd have been torn. She was also deeply in love with Roy Rogers at the time. Roy was okay, but he couldn't hold a candle to my Italian pilot.

One day Adriano came over to our house. Dolores must have been staying at our place, and he was coming to pick her up. Donna-Lee and I had been waiting for him to arrive, and when he drove up our driveway, we were ready for him. We had practiced impressing him with our great tumbling prowess. We performed daring flips and perfect cartwheels on the lawn where he would surely see us and be in awe of our amazing talent. I was two years older than my sister, and I knew that he couldn't help but notice that I was the superior tumbler. My sister wasn't quite as eager to win his love as I was, so her performance was a little half-hearted. I, on the other hand, had tumbled head over heels ten times in a row before I ran out of lawn space. Oh yes, head over heels!

As proof of his mutual love and adoration, he took us to Greenberg's Store for ice cream. I don't actually remember Dolores being there, but I guess she must have been. We sat at the soda fountain on round stools that we could spin on. Spinning stools, ice-cream, and Adriano. It was one of the greatest days of my life!

Dolores married Adriano and moved to Italy. Not long after they were married, he was killed in a plane crash.

CAROL DAHLSTROM

When she looks back on her childhood, Carol pictures herself as a sunny little girl with braids, moving through a sunny world. She says she feels fortunate to have grown up in the small ski town of Rossland in the interior of British Columbia in a stable, vibrant family. As a ten-year-old in the 1950s, she was, unlike children growing up in the twenty-first century, naïve about matters of love and romance—and certainly about sex.

The Most Handsome of Dentists

There's nothing more intense than a crush held by a ten-year-old girl. It's the awakening of the notion of romantic love, not to mention the first stirrings of the hormones that will play enormously during the next few years (and decades) of our lives. It will be many years before we settle on an appropriate object of these intense crushes. And there will be many painful romantic events along the way.

But I digress. My first true love was our family dentist, Dr. Sinclair, the most handsome man I could ever have imagined. He was divinely handsome. I was a budding singer when I was ten and would go around our house singing at the top of my lungs, over and over again, "I love you, Doctor Sinclair. I love you. I love you."

My brother (a year younger than I, and with absolutely no understanding of the intensity of my love) was incensed by my attempts at operatic expression and would stomp off to his bedroom to plan his revenge. His revenge was to start up his model airplane's gas-powered motor, which he had mounted on his dresser. Have you ever heard the sound of a model-airplane motor in a small house? It was more than adequate to drown out the sound of a little girl singing, even at the top of her lungs.

I don't remember my parents having had an opinion about my first true love. Perhaps they hadn't noticed. After all, they had their own issues. My mother had discovered a lump in her breast and had had it surgically removed. The lump turned out to be benign, but her recovery was difficult, at least from my perspective as a ten-year-old. During her recovery, I spent some time with the Sinclair family, and it was during that time that Dr. Sinclair kissed me. I am now an eighty-year-old woman, but I remember that kiss to this day. I remember that I was standing in the middle of the Sinclairs' kitchen. I wore a pale green-and-white striped dress. I was distraught about my mother, and Dr. Sinclair kissed me on the top of my head. He loved me!

I know now that it was not just Dr. Sinclair that I loved. I loved his family too. Dr. Sinclair's wife was a singer, and I adored her. Dr. Sinclair and his wife had produced three beautiful children (how could they not have done so?), and I adored those children.

Our families were close, and we shared a property at the Lake. One brilliant summer day when I had just turned eleven, it happened that I was left to catch a ride to the Lake with my beloved, just him and me in the car. He was driving, of course, and I sat in the passenger seat. He happened to place his hand on the seat between us. I know now that it was just a way of giving his hand a rest from the steering wheel. But my eleven-year-old self wondered, *What if I just placed my own hand on his and we became lovers, right then and there, in the middle of nowhere?* At that time in my life, I understood the definition of *lovers* to be a boy and a girl walking hand-in-hand into the forest and living happily ever after.

I didn't, of course, place my hand on his, and of course we didn't walk hand-in-hand into the forest, and it all worked out in the end. I grew up, as we all do, and in the process went on to love others, many of them equally as inappropriate as my first true love.

GUNNAR WAHLSTRÖM

Gunnar was born in Gothenburg, Sweden, and currently teaches at University of Gothenburg. He has been married for twenty-five years to Elisabeth, an engineer, and they have two children. He loves the sea, fishing, and engines, and even does his own boat and car maintenance. Even more impressive to me, he has been running eight kilometres a day, six days a week, for over thirty years.

Gunnar once startled his students by floating away into the past.

Floating Away with Hillivi

A couple of weeks ago I was meeting with students in my office, advising them on some aspects of their group project on auditor independence. When the session was over, we had a few minutes to kill before the next group arrived, and I asked one of the students, Annika, where she was from.

"Södertälje," she replied.

Södertälje!

Forty-five years disappeared. I was no longer sitting in my office in the twenty-first century. I was back in Södertälje, the town that holds my memory of Hillivi, of living next door to Hillivi.

We played together often. A passion had hit us. (Maybe passion is easier when we are younger.) There are some things that I have never forgotten: her hair, her laughter....

As I reminisced about Hillivi, transported out of my office, I was no longer responsible for the students who had come for my advice. But just then Annika's concerned voice interrupted my daydream.

"Are you ok, Gunnar?"

CARL PAUPTIT

Carl left school at the end of Grade 10, started working for $22.00 a week, and ended up with a legacy. I know all this because he's my cousin. At twenty-three, he started an instant printing business, Flash Reproductions, and some forty-five years later the Graphic Arts Association of Canada awarded him a Lifetime Achievement Award for his development of unique products. Carl and the people at Flash Reproductions have always adhered to a simple motto: "The person who says it can't be done is usually interrupted by someone doing it."

Falling in Love at Church Camp

Picture this setting: a ten-year-old farm boy away from home for ten days for the first time in his life. It was the summer of 1954, and I was attending a Bible camp on Prince Edward Island. My cousin Peter and I were recipients of this all-expense-paid experience, compliments of our Sunday School teacher. I'm not sure why we were chosen. Potential missionaries in the making, perhaps?

This was a camp for boys and girls, but the girls were in cabins a comfortable distance from us guys. Meals were served in a large unisex dining hall, but it was several days before we became comfortable with our newfound friends—especially the girls.

One morning, as we were about to leave the dining hall after a healthy breakfast, our leader made an announcement: For dinner that evening, every camper was to come to the table dressed in clothing from a member of the opposite sex. Peter and I were just starting to be comfortable enough to make new friends. But a girl? This was heavy stuff! Panic set in!

The whole camp was in turmoil! The girls were giggling, and the guys were—well, they were just being klutzy guys!

Peter and I decided to join forces in our effort to look cool and wander over to the girls' cabins. Then a miracle happened! (For me, not for Peter.) Before my very eyes, a beautiful girl with long, blonde hair was standing in front of me! I just stood there, giving myself instructions: "Be cool, Carl. She must see something in you. I bet it's your bright-red, curly hair. Say something, Stupid! What's happening to you? Your mother always said you had the gift of gab. Where is it when you need it?"

Finally, after what seemed forever, this beautiful, long-haired blonde said, "Hi. I'm Linda."

You'd think, after Linda taking the lead, I would calmly and coolly say, "Hi. I'm Carl." But no. I said, "Linda who?"

Fortunately, she didn't give up. "I'm Linda McCrae," she replied, with such class. Finally, I came to my senses and replied, "And I'm Carl Pauptit."

Linda and I chatted and traded stories, as magic overcame me. Poor Peter. I had forgotten he was standing there next to us. He finally gave up and wandered off. Then came the big question! Linda blurted out, "Would you trade clothing with me for dinner?"

Can you imagine? Linda McCrae wanted ME to wear her clothing!

The next five days at camp left me with enough memories for a lifetime. We spent every possible moment together, and I experienced my first kiss with someone other than my mother and my bulldog, Ben.

Thank you, Linda McCrae for the memories.

LINDA GRIJALVA

Linda is a retired hairstylist who lives in Tucson, Arizona, and is "having a blast playing pickleball and golfing." She loves retirement and spending time with her granddaughter, Isabelle.

Kissing and Telling

"Brace yourself!" I told Isabelle. "It wasn't your grandfather."

"How can that be?" she asked. "You and Gramps met when you were fourteen."

"Oh, but this happened in second grade, when I first met Mickey Pool (his real name)." He was the one, I was sure. Easy on the eyes, funny and fun—the whole package. I stalked Mickey through notes I never gave him and hang-up calls when I heard his voice on the phone. This romance ended with a kiss.

The day came when, during recess, Mickey started chasing me, and I ran as fast as I could. He was faster, and when he caught me, we both went down. That's when it happened. He kissed me on the cheek. I held that kiss all day and told my mother I would never, ever wash my cheek again. Moral of the story: Love can knock you down!

Isabelle laughed, and I told her, "There's more: True Love Number 2."

Fifth grade. His name was John. My parents and I were sitting in the car outside the skating rink.

"Look that's him. He's the one I love."

My parents gave me The Look. "The one with the long, blond hair?"

"Yes. That's him."

I skated with John and held his hand. At the end of the evening, he wanted to wait with me outside for my parents to pick me up, and I was hoping I might get my first kiss. (Isabelle looked surprised.) As we stood in the dark at the back of the rink, he asked if he could kiss me. I leaned in and closed my eyes and puckered up. Nothing happened.

He said, "Well, you have to open your eyes."

What? Weird.

I opened my eyes, and he leaned in and put his eyelashes on my eyelashes and batted his. I stepped back, surprised and disappointed.

"That's a butterfly kiss," he said.

"Moral of the story, Isabelle: There is more than one kind of kiss. More on that later. Now it's time to go to school. Have a great day and no kissing!"

* * *

First Love Number 3: Still in search of my first real kiss.

I met him at my first high school dance. I could tell he was sweet on me, and I thought he was sweet too. He swooped in and put his arm around my shoulder. He was in a grade higher than mine, which was important at the time. He asked if I wanted to go outside. We sat on the steps, and he leaned in and planted a big one on me. Wow! Yep, there were fireworks. Three years later, I said "I do" to my one true love, and we've been married for forty-seven years.

Moral of the story, Isabelle: A kiss can last a lifetime. And be prepared if you go outside: It could be anything from a butterfly kiss to a life-changing experience.

And no kissing, Isabelle, until you're twenty-five.

BEV CAMERON

Bev has played many roles in her full and interesting seventy-eight years. As an academic, she served as a professor, university administrator, and consultant. She describes herself as "a friend, sister, wife, mother, economist, animal lover, traveller, reader, cook, dual Canadian/US citizen, and more."

First Kindred Spirit

I lived in a rural area until the middle of Grade 4, when we moved into town, and I attended much larger schools. My rural school had two rooms—Grades 1 to 3 in one room and Grades 4 to 6 in the other.

I fell in love with Kenny in Grade 1. It was one of those things that happen when you meet a kindred soul. Neither of us was the nicest-looking child in the room; neither of us was the most athletic; neither of us had the best social skills. But what we did have seemed to click without our having to think about it. We were in the same grade; we liked many of the same things (like animals). I was the oldest in my family with younger siblings, and Kenny was the youngest with older sisters. It worked, and it was comfortable. We were the best of friends.

As we got a bit older, I remember talks about the future, going to university, getting married, and the like. Sometimes we held hands, but if we were seen, that led to teasing from other kids. There were a few secret kisses in some hidden part of the playground.

In the middle of Grade 4, my family moved to one of the two larger nearby towns. In spite of promises to keep in touch, our lives diverged, and only memories of a grade school love remain. Kenny's family continued living where they were, and he went to high school in the other large town. Michigan has two large state universities; I went to one and Kenny went to the other. I've seen Kenny only once since we parted seventy years ago. I know he became a veterinarian and opened a practice near the area where we both lived. I think he's been married three times. He didn't answer the Facebook message I sent him several months ago.

Whatever Kenny's current situation, I have fond memories of a first love and a good friend.

MARIE GRAHAM

Marie lives in Brandon, Manitoba; she is ninety-three. At age eighty-five, she "came out" as a poet to her family and a small group of friends. Wide areas of learning, music, community, humour, and finding trust are important aspects of her life. In 2019 she lost her real true love of nearly seventy years, Jack. Through this human experience, she learned that remembering, storytelling, and the reading of others' experiences are a caring balm at this stage in the arc of life.

True Love, First Kiss

What each of us means by true love may be different. Does it mean the first crush? The initial rush of sexual passion? The time we knew we wanted to be with someone the rest of our lives? The first kiss we wanted and experienced? For me it was my first kiss.

The culture of the times decreed that people didn't hug and kiss as easily as they do today, much less say, "I love you." Many children, including me, craved physical touch, and a first kiss was an entrance into romantic love.

When I was about ten, I lived on a rather poor, mixed, quarter-section farm. It was near the end of the Great Depression. Community members lived off the avails of their farms, and although we were poor, we didn't feel different from our neighbours. Making do and recycling was normal.

I walked the 1.25 miles to a small one-room school with my brother Johnny and four foster brothers—Eddy, Dennis, Davey, and Jano—who lived with a neighbour couple up the road. We did the many silly childhood playful things—teasing, chasing, pushing, rolling in the snow, and playing Anti-I-Over and catch.

We also played a game called Knife. We all had pocketknives. Because I was a girl, mine was a smaller pen knife with a white handle. We would squat in a circle around a piece of sandy or softened ground. The aim of the game was to take an open-bladed knife, put the point of the blade on a body part and flip the handle so that the knife somersaulted to stand with the blade in the dirt and the handle standing up. The knife was deemed to be "standing" if we could slide a finger under the handle and not touch the earth. If it fell flat, it was the next player's turn. We started by pointing the blade on a thumb. If that worked, we moved to the next finger, and, if successful, we progressed through our other digits to wrist, elbow, shoulder, and forehead. The winning place was the top of the head. This was a fun game and could take a long time to play.

Some of us had mouth organs, and we played popular songs like "You Are My Sunshine." Eddy liked to sing cowboy songs. And we could all whistle—even double whistle by positioning our tongues in our cheeks and vibrating them.

In the spring when the sap was running, we could cut a small, fat, finger-sized poplar and fashion a whistle. In winter we tried to snare rabbits or weasels because their pelts were worth small change. (But the luck was with the animals, not with us.) When school was out in summer, we would visit back and forth the half mile to jump in the hay loft, play tag, or pretend we were the characters we saw in the Saturday afternoon matinees in town. Sometimes we had noise-making caps for the toy pistols we carried in holsters or in our pockets. Firing them made the gangsters and sheriffs seem real.

All of this was platonic—kids playing together with the few resources that we had at our disposal. But I kind of liked Davey. He was about my age, and he was less pushy than his older two brothers. We seemed to gravitate toward each other.

At some point at school there were transient pairings of boys and girls. Davey's oldest brother paired with the oldest girl in school; he would put his arm around her waist, and sometimes they would kiss behind the school door. And I would wonder what it was like to be kissed.

One winter Davey's whole family came to our home for supper, and I was thinking about kissing him. I stood beside the tea-towel rack and pressed my lips onto the towel, thinking about Davey. And later it happened. We were behind the pantry wall, and he stood next to me and whispered, "K-I-S-S?" Then we kissed on our lips. It felt so soft and kind, probably more so to me, as a child who was touch deprived. I think we did it again before the evening was over. We considered ourselves boyfriend and girlfriend after that.

JACK HAUEN

Jack reports on Ontario politics for *The Trillium*. He lives in Toronto but is originally from the West Coast of Canada. He enjoys cooking, video games, and letting the Vancouver Canucks break his heart. And he thinks it is only fair to tell readers that he was published in this book through nepotism.

Dance Club

In Grade 6, I joined dance club because of a girl. I learned a full four minutes of choreography to Will Smith's "Gettin' Jiggy Wit It."

Practices were at 7 AM. I spent most of each practice watching her, to make sure she wasn't watching me. I was tired all the time.

I wrote her a poem after our performance. I gave it to her while wearing SpongeBob SquarePants pyjamas. (It was Pyjama Day at school.)

We didn't get jiggy wit it.

DIANE COOLEY

Diane taught elementary grades in Saskatchewan for several years before moving to Winnipeg with her family. Once her two daughters started school, she joined the Manitoba Department of Education, where she worked as a curriculum developer and program administrator for thirty years.

Last Week I Told My Husband About My Secret Love

His name was Donald. Or Malcolm. Or Callum. Or maybe all three. Obviously, a serious Scottish connection in that family. Perhaps it started in Grade 3, when he and I were singled out for a transfer to a more advanced Grade 3/4 class. Something about him set him apart from the other boys. Maybe his brown hair with a slight curl or his hazel eyes. Or the light sprinkling of freckles across his nose. I only know that I developed a crush that lasted for the next six years. It was kept alive by brief romantic encounters—the recess in Grade 5 when the boys captured me, so he could kiss me. (Was he a willing participant?) The Saturday afternoon at the skating rink when he held my hand for a few rounds of "The Skaters' Waltz."

Oh, there were brief diversions, when the dreamboat Mormon missionary, Elder Byron Todd, turned up on our doorstep, determined to convert unbelievers to his cause. (My mother probably suspected why I encouraged return visits.) Or fantasies prompted by the endless parade of American GIs who frequented our small town of Sioux Lookout near the US base on the Pine Tree Line. With their crew cuts, blue jeans, lazy drawls, and white T-shirts with cigarette packs bulging from their sleeves, they cut dashing figures right out of James Dean movies. But I remained steadfast to the end.

The fall I turned fourteen, my family moved from Sioux Lookout to Estevan. Sorting and packing for departure, I was closing one chapter of my life and looking forward to the next. But first...I clipped Donald's image from our Grade 8 class photo and enclosed it in my locket. This I buried at the foot of a tree on Mitchell's Point, a narrow finger jutting out into Pelican Lake. I guess the treasure is there still.

Memories of my first, secret love eventually faded, crowded out by the novelty of being the new girl in a new school and the start of a new love that continues to this day.

DANIEL PERLMAN

Dan is Professor Emeritus of Family Science at the University of British Columbia. From early childhood, he has been fascinated with the question of what makes relationships terrific and terrible; seventy years later, he has some answers and some mysteries still to be solved. Dan tells not only of his own preschool romance here; he summarizes research that provides some insight into romantic love in childhood.

Preschool Polygamy: My First Love Affair

I grew up just after World War II in a small American town, population five thousand. The population swelled in the summer with city folks who had summer cottages, and it shrank in the winter. In some ways it was a typical small town. In other ways, my town was unique. For a brief period, it had been headquarters for the Communist Party. Many residents were employed in the fine and performing arts—mainly artists, musicians, and writers.

Lots of people in the town, but not all, were pretty liberal—avant-garde you might say. My parents always thought sex was a nice and natural activity. My mom was an early childhood educator, and she wanted us to learn about our bodies, people being in love, and sex, in age-appropriate ways. As preschoolers, we had anatomically correct dolls and storybooks about how animals had babies—all explained at a three- or four-year-old level, of course.

As a child of two of the liberally minded parents in our town, I started my romantic career shortly after nursery school with Pixie and Jeannie. Pixie's mom and dad were artists, and Jeannie's dad was our Republican representative to the state assembly. Pixie and Jeannie were my first true loves. Whenever I had a chance to pick my playmates, I chose them. When we were separated, and I couldn't play with them, I became anxious, and I'd cry and plead with my mom to let me meet with them.

Pixie and Jeannie were the first girls I kissed. Here's how I remember it. There was a green space behind Jeannie's house. In the days before children needed an adult to walk them to school, we would play there by ourselves for hours. We would run around, and I would catch up to Pixie or Jeannie, smack a kiss on her face and run away, and we'd all giggle hilariously. In my 1940s male chauvinism, I remember being the kisser; I don't remember being kissed back.

After our first kisses, we went to elementary school together, but then our romance began to fade. I went away to high school. Pixie married fairly young, and I saw her once shortly after that. I saw her again at a dinner party when I was perhaps sixty. Otherwise, Pixie and Jeannie and I lost touch. But my memory of them is still warm and positive.

As an adult, I became a professor who studied close relationships, which gave me a chance to answer the question: "Was my first romantic experience precocious and atypical?" In the 1988 volume of the *Journal of Psychology and Human Sexuality*, eminent social psychologist Elaine Hatfield and her colleagues asked the question, "At what age do children first experience passionate love?" Some psychologists believe that a desire for bonding is hardwired into humans and is present virtually from birth. Others argue that because love is fuelled by adolescent hormonal changes, it kicks in only after puberty. To answer the question of when children first experience love, Hatfield asked a large sample of Hawaiians between four and eighteen years of age to agree or disagree with statements about love.

It turns out that my experience was typical of Hatfield's four-year-olds. She and her colleagues found that children as young as four—about my age when I first kissed Pixie and Jeannie—experience passionate love and have their first girlfriend or boyfriend. They asked the children in their study to select a boyfriend or girlfriend, which even four- and five-year-olds were able to do. And children that age said they "very much agreed" with such statements as, "I feel like things would always be sad and gloomy if I had to live without [Pixie or Jeannie] forever."

Overall, girls were into passionate love more than boys were, but this finding was qualified by age differences. Hatfield's boys (and I) were high in passionate love as four- and five-year-olds, but boys' level of passion declined, only to rise again following puberty. (My next girlfriend was Cynthia when I was fifteen or sixteen.) The passionate love pattern for girls wasn't as clear; it didn't decrease as noticeably in the elementary school years.

You may wonder if I was equally in love with Pixie and Jeannie. Me, too. I bonded to Pixie first (I don't think Jeannie was in my earliest preschool), so we had a longer and perhaps more prominent relationship. After preschool, I gave up polygamy and I am now passionately in love with a wonderful wife. When I kiss her, she kisses me back.

BARBARA CZARNIAWSKA

Barbara was born December 1948 in Bialystok, Poland, where her family moved from Vilnius after World War II. She is Professor Emerita at Gothenburg University and has been a Swedish citizen since August 1988. Barbara's story reinforces Hatfield's research on romance among five-year-olds.

The Red Bag: A Love Story

When I was five, a man came to visit my father. He brought his son, Marek, who was my age. Marek had pretty, dark, curly hair, and I thought him to be extremely handsome. His father gave me a red handbag, saying it was a gift from his son to me. The handbag was bright red (do you know a lovelier colour?) and was not unlike the one that Mrs. Thatcher used to sport in her good days: It could stand by itself, and it had a metal clasp and a round handle. It remained my only handbag in years to come.

In some pictures taken during my summers in the countryside, I can be seen with my country girlfriends, who were allowed to take turns being photographed with my handbag—with me always in the picture, smiling a sophisticated, big-city smile. None of them had a handbag! (I know that in North America, girls get handbags in their infancy, but this was old Europe, circa 1953.)

A year later, I started school, and Marek was in the same class. He was still handsome, but it was already known that he was a baddie. Gossiping among ourselves, we decided that he would certainly become a hooligan or perhaps even a criminal. My parents said that his father might have wanted Marek and me to become friends so I could have a good influence on him, but we never had any more personal contact.

Children's Loves

I found a boy on Facebook with his name. He could be his grandchild. He looks a bit like him.

Was I in love with Marek or the red handbag, do you think? To help you in helping me answer this difficult question, I am attaching a photo of me and my friends and the red handbag—in black and white because such were photos then.

At any rate, our love was never formalized. It was only later, when I was seven, that I got engaged for the first and last time in my life—to a guy named Staszek in Warsaw—and got a ring! So, which one counts? Marek? Staszek? Or the red handbag?

BJØRN ERIK RAMTVEDT

Bjørn Erik is a Norwegian psychologist and researcher in his sixties. On the personal side, his path leads to dreamwork and meditation. Bjørn Erik provides us with a third story of a five-year-old's romance.

A Healing Love at Five

I met my first love in early summer 1962, at the age of five. I saw her for the first time outside our neighbours' house, on my way down the road to meet with one of my friends. I fell in love then and there. She looked like an angel, and I almost levitated as my eyes took her in. Her appearance caressed my heart and soul.

The beauty and tender presence she radiated evoked feelings and a state of mind I had never experienced and that totally transformed my behaviour. I used to be a shy child. When the older boys had teased me about having a girlfriend because I occasionally spent time with a girl that lived nearby, I felt embarrassed. Now shyness and embarrassment were nonexistent.

The next day I walked straight over to the neighbours' house and asked about the girl. My neighbour told me that her name was Nina, that she was one year older than I was, and that she practiced ballet. But most important, I was informed that Nina went to the two-year kindergarten that I would start that fall.

Kindergarten started up again in August, and there was Nina. I immediately expressed my love for her without hesitation or shyness. I felt invulnerable. No comments from anyone could change my state of mind or stop me. I was proud of my feelings for Nina and confident in my mission to protect her and take care of her any way I was able. I had no concern about rejection, although I did fight with other boys to make them stay away from her. Fortunately, only one of the boys was stronger than I was, but he was interested in another girl.

One day the boys in kindergarten participated in a competition arranged by the staff. One boy after another had to take a bat and hit a wooden barrel filled with oranges, in an attempt to break the barrel, so all the oranges would fall out. I was the one who succeeded. The reward was to choose the girl that I wanted to sit by my side during a feast in the kindergarten. And Nina was happy to be chosen by me. Some months later, she invited me to her birthday party. I felt honoured.

But life goes on. Because she was one year older than I was, she started primary school the next fall, while I remained in kindergarten. And before I started primary school, my family moved to another town far from Oslo, and I never saw her again. I am left with a photo of Nina and me, sitting next to each other in kindergarten. Looking at this photo today, I still see why, as a five-year-old kid, I fell in love with her. She evoked the heroic archetype in me.

Nina: born May 1956. We spent a year together in Hoff Kindergarten in Oslo from August 1962 to June 1963. My time with her was a healing experience and remains a powerful memory.

Teenage Loves

> Nobody, she felt, understood her.
>
> Not her mother, not her father, not her sister or brother, none of the girls or boys at school.
>
> Nadie, except her man.
>
> - Raquel Cepeda

I was walking along a path in the golf course in Oro Valley, Arizona—not golfing, just walking—listening to *Paul Anka's 21 Greatest Hits* on my iPhone. One of my 1960 favourites, "Puppy Love," came on, and I began to wonder if there were other songs with the same theme. So I cut my walk short, came straight back to my computer, and entered "songs about puppy love" into Google. I got 48.5 million hits. And I learned that there are apparently 1,300 lyrics, 200 artists, and 50 albums matching those key words.

I told my friend Marek Opaliński (who describes himself merely as an obscure Polish lawyer) about gathering stories for *My First True Love*, and he recounted a conversation he had recently had with a friend, in which they were philosophizing about teenage romance:

> We had a general discussion about love and feelings, and we looked back to a time when we were younger and decided that at seventeen, eighteen, or nineteen, love was one of the most important issues in our lives. The whole discussion ended with a conclusion: We can never underestimate the seriousness of first love, and, as parents, we can never cheer up our teenagers by saying, "You'll see in the future that there will be more important things later in life." Because for them (and for us) it is (and was) an extremely important issue.

I couldn't agree more—nor could the many psychologists, poets, novelists, and screenwriters for whom teenage love formed the subject of their scientific and literary contributions. Not to forget the 200 singers who have sung 1,300 songs and recorded 50 albums about puppy love and the songwriters who wrote those songs.

AUDREY INGÓLFSDÓTTIR

Audrey is an academic, writer, lecturer, and globe trotter, whose home base is Iceland. She is passionate about anything related to self-empowerment, sustainability, or social responsibility, and she dreams of a world with greater harmony between humans and nature. She enjoys being out in nature and is also an avid runner.

When Love Isn't Enough

I met him again on Facebook five years ago. When we reconnected, I hadn't seen or talked to him for more than sixteen years, and it was more than ten years since I'd heard any news about him. He was my first love, and I was happy to reconnect and be able to follow how he was doing. But I was also curious to find out what had happened to him.

I still don't know the entire story, but he seems to have lost his way. His Facebook profile is filled with links to videos about conspiracy theories, with an occasional reference to God and the Bible. In the few private messages we shared, he has admitted to having suffered from Post-Traumatic Stress Disorder related to his service in the army, and I've discovered from some of his online posts that not only did his marriage fall apart, but that he isn't allowed to see or interact with his only daughter. I don't know the reason, but reading between the lines, my fear is that violence played a role.

* * *

We met when I was eighteen. He had dark hair and beautiful brown eyes. When he looked at me, I felt like something melted inside. I could tell from the beginning that he was curious about me, and I found him incredibly handsome and charming. But I was too shy even to start a conversation.

It was three years later that we became a couple, when I came back to the USA for my university studies. We dated my first winter in university, and when we first kissed, I felt like the happiest girl on the planet. He was warm and gentle, and he told me all his most sensitive secrets.

A few weeks after we started our relationship, he took me for a drive in a neighbourhood I had never visited before. I don't remember where it was, but there were many large houses. I was a little bored, and I didn't understand why we were driving around. Then he stopped the car, looked at me, and said with determination in his voice, "One day I'm going to have a house like this. One day I'm going to be rich."

I still remember my amazement. This was obviously something extremely important to him, but for me the goal of becoming rich enough to be able to buy a big house was about the most uninspiring goal I could imagine. I knew I was heading somewhere different in my life. This moment is still vivid in my memory. Even though I was still emotionally involved in the relationship, I knew from that moment that our journey together would not be a long one. Our dreams were too different. It still took some months for our relationship to end, and it did involve some pain to let him go. But the awareness that this love never had the potential of a long-term relationship made the breakup easier.

Regardless of our short time together, he still has a place in my heart. I wish him well, and I'm sad to see how his life has developed. He didn't get rich, and I don't think he owns a big house, but that isn't the part that I'm sad about. I am sad to see that he has not only lost the relationships that were most important to him, but that also, at times, he seems to have lost his sense of reality. Yet, I find it strangely calming to see his frequent and often odd posts online. At least he is alive, and I know where he is. And perhaps one day he will find peace again.

KELLY ARNDT

Kelly is an international educator who has lived in Europe, Asia, Africa, and South America, where she taught teenagers in various schools. Although her fantastical first love brought her a reprieve from growing pains, she found the real thing with her husband Simon, also an international educator. Longer vacations usually take them back to their home in Brugge, Belgium or to visit family in Canada.

#4

My first love was #4. My #4 was a hockey player. He wasn't the original #4, but he was my #4, and I loved everything about #4 without ever knowing him.

Growing up where I did—in Wetaskiwin, Alberta—meant having the world's greatest hockey team as my team. And being a teenage girl at a time when girls didn't play hockey, the only way I could love the game was as a spectator. And as a romantic fourteen-year-old, I wanted to be swept away by a rich, handsome, older man, so my #4 played this role. I wanted to be rescued from the normal middle-class life I was living.

I had the posters on my wall. I had newspaper clippings that featured him. I had a jersey with #4 stamped on it. My love for #4 was not silent. I wasn't ashamed of it. My friends, classmates, and family all knew how I worshipped #4. Classmates went to games and took pictures of #4 in the pre-game, developed them, and gave them to me. I still have these photos.

But I was silent about how this first love played out in my mind. It took place at night before I fell asleep—a time to relax and let myself imagine. I created fictional worlds where #4 and I were madly in love. In my stories, our life together was noble and pure. I would keep one story line going for months. It was a serial in my mind, and each night I would pick up the story and further it until I fell asleep. They all started with how we would meet and move on to our courtship and eventual marriage. Once we were married and maybe had a child or two, I would start all over again. I loved the start of the story when we first met. I had us meeting during a snowstorm, where we were trapped in a lonely cabin, having to survive. I had us meeting as I bumped into #4 at a mall. I had us meeting when #4 hit me with his car and had to rush me to the hospital.

The three times I spoke to #4 during this period added nothing to my story. I couldn't say anything to him beyond "Hello." Before falling asleep in my bed, I was always eloquent or intelligent or cheeky or flirty—or all four together. I would woo him with my words. But in reality, I was a bedazzled teenager standing in front of a professional athlete ten years my senior.

But reality was not important. The dream life I had created with my #4 continued into college. I was older then, of course, and there would be real opportunities to meet—maybe at a bar or a restaurant. The stories grew with my experiences.

Then it ended—dramatically—in 1989. I was nineteen and in Australia on a student exchange. I phoned my father—the first time I had spoken to him since I left home four weeks earlier.

#4 was engaged.

My stories fractured and died. There was no way I could work with this detail—the reality of the situation closed every story option. I could not imagine how to work around the fact of his impending marriage. I went to my room, put away the picture of #4 I had brought with me, and cried.

SYLVIA ANDERSON KOSHYK

Sylvia is a retired nurse who spent twenty-four years at Children's Hospital in Winnipeg, first nursing in the Infectious Disease Ward and then serving as a paediatric operating room nurse. She has three children and an assortment of grandchildren, great-grandchildren, and grand-dogs. She describes herself (and her friends and family are quick to confirm this) as "someone who gets homesick if I go too far away from my house and family."

The Circuitous Route

There I was in late August 1955, taking the bus to Lundar, Manitoba, to begin permit teaching in a one-room school in the tiny, remote farming community of Lily Bay. I was seventeen, and for the first time in my life, I was moving away from my seven siblings, my parents, and my home on the edge of Netley–Libau Marsh. I was a shy, skinny girl, and I was homesick before the bus even left Winnipeg.

I had finished Grade 11 in Libau West School the year before, and that summer I had taken a six-week permit teacher's course at the Provincial Normal School in Winnipeg. I was then a qualified permit teacher. I had signed up for—or been sentenced to—a school year of teaching in Lily Bay. I felt no special calling to the teaching profession. The matter was more pragmatic. As one of the elder four of eight children, I had to earn some money to relieve my parents' struggle to clothe and feed us all. But, just as important was the need to get away from home territory, where every eligible male was either a brother or a cousin. I had read enough in my elder cousin's discarded copies of *True Story* magazine to know that a true love awaited me in the world beyond, and that my mission as a young woman of the 1950s was to get out there and nab that prize. And then *presto*, my life would be complete.

For the bus ride to Lundar, I had dressed in what must have been Libau farm-girl chic, including long white gloves. Long white gloves! I have no idea why I was wearing them. It was August, so it wasn't cold. Perhaps it was to cover the tremor in my hand as I brushed away the odd tear or as I placed a cigarette in my mouth. (Yes, I was smoking a cigarette! Why? Perhaps to show how cool I was. In any case, it was my first cigarette ever—and my last.) Or, more likely, the gloved hands fit my image of what a young lady would wear as she set off on a journey into the wide world, where true love awaited her.

Eventually, the bus pulled up at the Lundar Grocery Store, where I was to meet the people I would board with for the school year. The store must have been having a one-day sale on men's boots because it was crowded with men trying on and buying knee boots. There was potential for meeting my new love right there, I calculated. But then horror set in. I suddenly realized I'd need to ask for some feminine hygiene products before I went to the outback that was Lily Bay. I crept up to the counter and whispered that I needed some *Kotex*. The large, middle-aged grocer widened his eyes at me and shouted "KOTEX?" The knee-boot contingent stopped fitting and buying and stared at me. The grocer, wielding a large prod of some sort, knocked a box of *Kotex* off the top shelf, and it promptly fell down on my head. Now every person in the store was gawking at me. My initial appearance in their community as the new, eligible female hadn't gone as I had imagined.

But I did get through my year of teaching in spite of my continuing homesickness. There were eight children enrolled in Lily Bay School that year, and I badly wanted my students to learn and to enjoy learning. Some of them were extremely bright, some needed a great deal of help, and they all loved to be read to. So I did what I was born to do: I read books to them. I read more than I taught core subjects. I had a captive audience that sat as still as mice and hung onto my every word. I believe that a whole new world opened up to each and every one of them, a world where Black Beauty was alive.

The young permit teachers, most of whom were female, usually lived with a family in the community. I lived with the family of one of my Grade 8 students, and she and I walked over a mile to school together, a journey that was fraught with danger all year long. The legal deer-hunting season plus illegal poaching made the hunting season last all year in Lily Bay and environs, and we were always afraid that one or more of the mighty hunters would be silently lurking ahead of or beside us. I often turned my black parka inside out and walked in lockstep with my student, hoping that the red lining would identify us as humans before any hunter fired. But no accidental shooting of teachers or students in Lily Bay was recorded that year or ever since.

The other form of hunting was of more immediate interest to me. There was a number of single males in the community, which created the perfect storm of boy meets girl and an ideal opportunity for new love to flourish. I had no experience in the art of dating and feared that the opportunity for finding my first love might pass me by. Yet, against all odds, I did go out on dates while I was in Lily Bay. The hunt was on.

My first date was with a local farmhand who worked for the family I boarded with. I guess I fit the local criteria—I was female and single—so I was fair game. This man was extremely shy, but he somehow indicated to me and to the father and mother of the family I boarded with that there was a dance in Lundar, that Andy Dejarlis and his band were playing, and that he was going. The parents declared that they were too old and that their children were too young to go. So that left me. I dressed up and went to the dance with him. I enjoyed the music and danced with several single men, including a considerably older man who was looking for a wife, any wife, seeing that age was creeping up on him and his hair was falling out. I dodged his advances and observed the unspoken custom of those days, dancing with the "guy who brung me." But first love did not blossom there. Shortly after our date, he left Lily Bay to go "cutting wood up North."

My second Lily Bay date was with a local guy who worked in Winnipeg. He had his own car and drove with his left hand on the steering wheel and his right arm around my shoulder. He said that God had made him left-handed so he could drive while making out with his right hand. Certainly a cool dude, but there was no spark, no flame. We laughed, I met his mother (who was a distant relative), and we became friends. Then he returned to Winnipeg and his job, and we never dated again.

My third Lily Bay date was with a brother of the left-handed guy. He was a perfect Icelandic Viking type and a most beautiful man—blond hair, blue eyes, and a soft, gentle voice. He also had his own car! There was definite potential there, I thought. Our initial date was my idea of heaven. We went to a movie at the drive-in theatre, he put his arm around me as we watched the movie, we had a grown-up conversation after the movie finished, and we shared a goodnight kiss when he drove me home.

On the second date, we went out with some of his friends. By then, I had an enormous crush on Mr. Perfect. Just two dates and I was already imagining myself as his steady girlfriend. I felt like I was on a precipice, where plunging into first true love was just a matter of leaning over the edge and falling.

Alas, this man, this object of my adoration, went back to his job in Winnipeg and the girls who waited for him there. My courting days in that community were over. I left Lily Bay, I never smoked again, and I never taught school again. I returned to my known world of home and family, with the sting of the abrupt ending of that first crush lasting for some time—until I met Peter, that is.

I got a job in Winnipeg and returned home on the weekends, where one day in 1956 at a wedding anniversary social, I met Peter, a local farm boy who had grown up seven miles from my home place. He was tall and irresistible, and I soon forgot all about the world beyond. I married my home-grown treasure two years later, just after I turned twenty. I became a mother of three by 1964 and a nurse in 1972. Life has been great. Peter and I celebrated our sixtieth-fifth wedding anniversary in 2023, proving that the journey to find a true love can be a circuitous route that takes you back to where you started.

IRENE WAY

Irene is from Newfoundland but has lived in Nunavut; all across Canada; and in Xiian, China. She sees herself as an adventurer with a keen interest in all cultures, having spent time as a teacher in remote settlements in the Canadian Arctic many years ago and recently returning to Nunavut to work as a psychiatric nurse. She and her husband, Colin, have raised eight children, all of whom she describes as "delightful," and they're now settled in the prairie town of Selkirk, Manitoba, near their grandchildren. Irene's great pleasure is to "write about the experiences life has so kindly presented."

Forbidden Love
1963

He stood in a group of thirteen-year-old boys with his hands in his pockets, his black hair gleaming under the gymnasium lights. He wasn't the tallest or the best looking of the group, his movements uncertain as he shuffled from one foot to another, but he had a strong jaw and perfect indentations of dimples when he smiled. I had watched him all though grade school, his goodness, tolerance, and patience engaging my interest.

He glanced across the gym toward our group of giggling girls. I tried not to notice and looked down at my first pair of low heels with pointed toes, which were crushing my feet. The back of my neck felt prickly, and my hands began to sweat. Joan was asking me if my mother had made my burnished-gold, gathered skirt. I looked up, but my throat closed as I observed Paul gazing at me across the length of the gym, at this first fall dance, dedicated to the new batch of high-school Freshies.

Paul's eyes connected with mine for no more than a few seconds before we both lowered our heads. Adrenaline, dopamine, and serotonin rushed to the forefront of my brain, causing my heart to hammer as I struggled to attend to the nervous conversation of my girlfriends. The hushed dialogue was sprinkled with just enough laughter to keep the boys on the other side of the gym.

The chaperones on duty were attempting to get the dance started by calling upon some poor kids to dance with them, but nothing could change the proper protocol here: the meaningful glances to test the waters, the waiting for groups to break up so a boy could take the plunge, crossing the gym to invite a girl to dance. The initiator was usually the school jock, and no girl would refuse him. Once he made his move, other boys would cross the floor, each one vulnerable to a negative reply from the girl of his choice. As the ritual began, every girl's worst fear was that the boy she cared for would ask the girl next to her to dance. Then the negotiations began. Should she take a mate of lesser value or chance being left with no partner? This mating ritual took due time, no matter how the chaperones tried to rush the foreplay.

Finally big, blond Ted from the soccer team strutted across the gym. You could hear the sighs of relief as all eyes followed his path to Patricia, the cheerleader with the long blonde hair and the short, silver Twiggy dress. They moved to the dance floor, setting in motion a string of movement across the gym, as other boys sought partners.

I saw Paul advance toward our group of girls, but protocol indicated that I not give him any encouragement. As he closed in, I flushed, my mouth dry and my heart racing fast enough that I felt I was living my whole life in this one night. He touched my arm, and I jumped at the searing, exquisite pain of new love. I looked up into that pair of intense green eyes, and the world melted away. I could see the beads of sweat dripping from his hairline with one dark lock dangling the length of his forehead. Riveted to the spot, my senses heightened, my mouth finally unstuck, I whispered, "OK." He held out his hand, and I laid my hand in his, as we moved to the dance floor.

Paul placed his hand on the small of my back, and the band played "The House of the Rising Sun." I knew from that moment on that I would never follow my family's plan for me to become a nun. The thought of not ever feeling this vulnerability mixed with the sweet intenseness of the senses that made up romantic love was unbearable. A smile lingered on my lips. I knew this was my reason to fight the family verdict of my being sacrificed to the nunnery.

On the dance floor, we moved in relaxed unison, keeping the appropriate space between us so as not to alert the chaperones. My heels made our heights equal, and as he moved his head over my shoulder, our ears came together and melded with sweat. Time stopped, and on the cusp of womanhood, I now knew my true calling. It was love. I would love this boy, not yet a man, fiercely and well. The rest of life would happen, but I would always remember this passion of first love.

Paul and I danced together many times that evening, and as our first school dance ended, he was by my side, asking to walk me home. We talked a lot about nothing, laughed at the face in the full moon, and held hands tightly in the cool autumn air. Too soon we were at my home, standing outside the front door. He leaned in and offered the most delicious of slow, languid kisses. Then he whispered in my ear, "I have a calling to the priesthood." As my whole world crashed around me, he walked down the driveway, around the corner, and away from me. I stood for a long time on the front step, wondering if I had heard right but knowing that I had.

Finally, in Scarlet O'Hara fashion, raising my fist to the moon, not daring to address our God, I shouted at the moon above, the sound echoing down the empty street, "Why would you take him? Why? There are so many." The answer was as clear as if it were written in bold letters across the moon: "You won't come, but he will."

That first year of high school I danced with Paul many times, but I knew it would end. His attraction was his kindness, compassion, and peaceful calm, those same attributes that made the perfect priest. I made peace with the fact that he was not mine, and when Ted began to look my way, I moved quickly on to other loves.

* * *

1978

My husband and I were on a family visit from Ontario, back home to St. John's, Newfoundland, with our two small children. My older brother, Wayne, was now initiated into the priesthood. We all packed into Dad's new, black Parisian to attend a clerical celebration at the huge cathedral. The bishop was to address some seventy priests and seminarians from across the island. Families and visitors were wedged in the last half of the pews as the service began. The deep vigour of male voices in song made an impressive opening, followed by four spiritual female dancers dressed in flimsy chiffon gowns moving seductively to sacred music. I knew of the church's attempts to update, and spiritual dancers were now in vogue, but it looked to me like they were just teasing a multitude of starving men.

As the service drew to a close, the priests followed the bishop down the middle aisle in a flurry of incense. We watched for my brother, Wayne, and as he passed by, I saw the changes: His hair was a little shorter, and he'd put on weight. Mum would be happy, as her greatest worry was that he would go hungry with the business of priestly duties taking up all his time.

And then it happened. Paul walked by. The green eyes, the lock of gleaming, black hair dangling on his forehead. I was a child again, and Paul was walking across the gym. Our glances collided, and a slow smile spread across his strong jaw. And there were the dimples. He had filled out and was taller, but I saw the boy in the man. His gaze swept over the children and on to my husband before it settled again on me. He nodded, as did I, and the moment disappeared in time.

I will always be grateful to Father Paul, my first love.

My First True Love

LES RANKIN

Les was raised on a mixed farm in Western Manitoba, where he developed love and respect for nature and agriculture. After a career in Agribusiness, he now enjoys retirement with his wife, Diane, and pursues interests in short-story writing, photography, horticulture, cycling, and bridge playing with friends.

Runaway Love

My first love was not only gorgeous, but graceful in every respect. From my pre-teen perspective, she was perfect: liquid eyes; soft, pouty lips; and midnight-coloured hair that shone like wet coal when she flirtatiously tossed her head. As we walked together one sultry evening, I ramped up my courage and gave her a firm, but affectionate slap on her buttocks, not quite knowing how it would be received. Dina snorted once, farted twice, and then charged across the pasture as though she were running the Kentucky Derby, her black mane flowing freely, and her long tail arched high. My first love, a beauty to behold.

HERVÉ CORVELLEC

Hervé was brought up on the French Riviera in the 1960s and 1970s, then studied in Paris, and moved as a young man to Malmö in Southern Sweden. He still lives there with his wife and daughter, his two elder children having moved on to lives of their own. He has made an academic career in the field of organization studies, mostly at Lund University. During the years since his relationship with his first love ended, Hervé has retained a taste for Bach, the French reefer coat called *caban*, and swimming in the sea. And he assures me that he has become a better cook.

Things Forgotten, One Remembers

We were fifteen and attending different classes at the Lycée Albert I in Monaco. We had known each other for over a year and had kissed for the first time on Christmas Day, out on a small, nearby cape called *La pointe des douaniers*—I could show you the exact spot on Google View. Agreeing to meet on Christmas Day was probably a mutual "yes" in advance—maybe, I don't know. Anyway, I was so obviously overwhelmed by our newfound nearness that when I came back home later that afternoon, my mother asked me why I was so strange, possibly wondering if I had been drinking, which I hadn't been. Except that I might have been drinking the nectar of love, as cheap verses say.

We spent three emotional years discovering the first Other of our choice through endless talking along streets and beaches and in mountain lifts or doing the kinds of things that our parents erroneously thought were merely a teenage waste of time, like listening to the same songs together over and over again—John Lennon and Georges Brassens.

But studies took me to Paris, while she remained on the Riviera, and our story turned into a homemade Nouvelle Vague film about *amour* slowly ending to rhyme with *toujours*.

Beware of rhymes, *belle jeunesse*. Their stable harmony is delusive. Attempts at getting together again did not bring back our first sentiments. And we lost contact. Several years later, my mother told me that, in an imprecise past, she had seen her pushing a pram. Then my parents moved. And I have been to Monaco only once since.

I remember so much of her, if only I will. Moves of her shoulders, ways of chuckling, puzzling hesitations. Fractals that tell so much. Yet I had not given her a thought for years before Nina asked me to write these few lines.

Loves That Lasted

John Anderson my jo, John,
When we were first acquent,
Your locks were like the raven,
Your bonnie brow was brent;
But now your brow is bald, John,
Your locks are like the snaw;
But blessings on your frosty pow
John Anderson, my jo.

John Anderson my jo, John,
We clamb the hill thegither;
And monie a cantie day, John,
We've had wi' ane anither:
Now we maun totter down, John,
And hand in hand we'll go,
And sleep thegither at the foot,
John Anderson, my jo.

- Robert Burns

When I first thought about compiling stories for this book, I assumed that most of them would be about long-term relationships—stories that began in youth and extended into middle or old age. But stories of that type were surprisingly few. Several people in their sixties or seventies answered my call, but merely to tell me that they couldn't write a story for me—that their stories were too simple, too plain, too private, or too ordinary. They said such things as:

- I had a first true love, and he was my only true love.
- I feel blessed to still be in love with my first true love.
- I did have a first love, and he just happens to be my current love.
- She's the only person I ever wanted to be with in a committed relationship. I'm boring.

There were, however, ten people who told me—and now you—about their lasting love.

HAZEL COLWILL

This next story has a special place in my heart. It was written by my Aunt Hazel, who died at the age of one hundred. Along with the key roles she played on the family farm on Prince Edward Island, Hazel was a teacher, writer, visual artist, mother, grandmother, great-grandmother, and beloved aunt to many of us. And yes, Aunt Hazel, as you anticipated when you sent me your love story at the age of ninety-eight, you were the oldest person to write for this book.

The Best Christmas Gift Ever

I am probably the oldest person to contribute to this project. I was born in 1917, and my love story goes back to 1939. I was a young, inexperienced teacher, looking without success for a teaching position. My sister Jessie had made friends with a girl named Reta at sewing classes a few years earlier, and they had been corresponding. Reta wrote that her community was searching for a teacher, and in July 1939, Jessie, my father, and I drove sixty miles to Tyne Valley, PEI, to learn more about the job.

The first stop we made was at the farm where Reta lived. The school trustees were responsible for hiring teachers, and Reta's father, Woodland Colwill, was one of the school trustees. Mr. Colwill came with us to the homes of the other trustees, and in no time I was hired to teach in a one-room rural school of ten grades, beginning in August 1939.

Reta invited us back to the family farm for a delicious dinner. Her father was a widower. Joining us at the dinner table were four young adults: two girls with red hair—Una and Reta—and two men who had come in from repairing fences in the field. One of the men, Bill (Nina's father), had red hair. I assumed the other man, a tall, slim, dark-haired man named Claude, who didn't look like the others, was the hired man. Claude came to play an important role in my life.

After dinner, Mr. Colwill suggested that we stop at the neighbouring farmhouse to arrange for my room and board. This home, belonging to the Dyments, was close to the school, and I arranged to board with this fine family.

I agreed to take the teaching position and agreed to start teaching mid-August, which allowed for a two-week holiday in October so the children could help with potato digging. We didn't know it then, but mid-August turned out to be two weeks before the beginning of World War II—a time that became stressful for everyone.

My First *True Love*

The first Sunday I lived there, I went to church with the Dyments. Few families had a car in those days, and few roads were paved. The church was three miles away, and we went in a horse-drawn carriage. After that, I was invited to drive in the Colwill's family car.

I learned that Claude, the tall, slim, dark-haired man I had met on my first day in this community was not the hired man but was Mr. Colwill's son. One Sunday evening, Claude dropped in at the Dyment's house and asked me to go for a drive. When I said I was going to church, he offered to take the younger Dyment couple and me to church. This was our first date and the beginning of our relationship.

Soon Claude was a regular visitor at the house where I boarded. Because he lived just across the field, and neighbouring farmers worked together at some tasks, he could pretend he was coming over to talk about farming and still get a chance to talk to me. As time went on and we felt more comfortable with our relationship, everyone came to know the real reason for his visits.

I taught in Tyne Valley for the 1939–1940 school year, and by the time the year was over, Claude and I were quite taken with each other. Claude had won my heart in a way that had never happened before. He was my *first true love*.

The next school year, 1940–1941, I taught school in the community where I had grown up. It was important to Claude and me to see if this mutual attraction would remain with distance between us. In those days, travelling sixty miles was much more difficult than it is today. There were few cars, and trains or a horse with wagon or sleigh were still the most common modes of travel. Most roads were impassable during the winter months or during the spring mud season.

Claude and I wrote letters back and forth when we could, but he had gone to work in the lumber woods in another province to "make some extra money," so the letters were infrequent. Just before Christmas, Claude returned to PEI and boarded a train from his home, arriving at a train station six miles from my home. And although he didn't know the area, he walked those six miles on a cold winter's night just to see me. When he arrived at our house, he asked me to marry him, and when I said, "Yes," he presented me with a diamond ring. I learned that the "extra money" he had earned was for my ring. It was the best Christmas surprise I ever had! During Claude's visit, we made plans to be married when school closed.

On July 9, 1941, my all-time favourite minister married us in the church manse. Because it was wartime, our wedding was a quiet event, and that suited us perfectly. My sister Jessie and her husband-to-be, Robert, were our only witnesses. This was a happy day for us.

After an overnight honeymoon, we went to live in the farmhouse I had visited just two years earlier. There were many changes in this family that year. Claude's brothers, Bill and Earle, had joined the Canadian Armed Services. Four of my father-in-law's children—Earle, Claude, Reta, and Una—were married in 1941, and Bill married in 1942. Now there was just my father-in-law living on the farm with the newlyweds—Claude and me. My father-in-law was welcoming and kind to me and, later, to our children.

Within ten years, we had four children: Judy, Emily, Linda, and John. What a busy household! There were seven people at our table for three meals a day, and extra places were sometimes set for men who were working on the farm or extended family members visiting their former home.

Claude and I worked hard on the farm, for there was always work to do. We grew most of our food. I prepared our fresh food from scratch, and it was always tasty. My daily chores included cleaning the house, making bread, churning butter, and washing the many parts of the separator—a manual machine used twice a day to separate the milk from the cream. I washed our clothes on a washboard, hung them on a line to dry, and ironed with a sad iron—a delta-shaped iron slab with a handle that was set upon the wood stove to heat to the desired temperature. Hardly an exact science. Seasonal jobs included spring cleaning, gardening, haying, and potato planting and digging.

Claude worked from dawn to dusk, but he loved the farm and he loved farming. We worked as a team, got along well, and we didn't have time to disagree. When our children were old enough, we gave them daily chores to help teach them the skills they needed for life.

Everyone welcomed the end of World War II. The soldiers came home, and life began to change rather quickly. Farm work got somewhat easier with the switch from horses to tractors. When we got electricity, we bought a milking machine for Claude to help with the twice-a-day milking chores and a labour-saving washing machine for me. As our children got older, we felt it was time for me to return to teaching.

The years went by quickly. Our children grew up and married good spouses. Within a few years, we had twelve grandchildren. They enjoyed family get-togethers in the farmhouse, and we certainly enjoyed them. They became the fifth generation that had played, laughed, worked on, and loved this farm and this dear old house. Now I am the proud great-grandmother of twenty-four great-grandchildren.

I have seen numerous changes in my lifetime, but my family has brought me my greatest joy. I have been a widow now for several years, but I have only fond memories of our sixty years of married life. This remarkable love story all began because I was looking for a teaching position to begin my career. And here in this community, I had the opportunity to meet Claude, the man who was to become my husband and lifelong love.

FRED STARKE

Fred is a retired professor who worked in the Asper School of Business at the University of Manitoba from 1968 to 2007. He was born and raised in the USA, but moved to Canada in 1968, when he was twenty-six years old. His main reason for coming to Canada, he tells me, was to go fishing, but he ended up having a career in Canada as a professor and academic administrator. Besides fishing, his hobbies are growing flowers in his greenhouse and singing in gospel quartets.

The First Week of December

I lived in the city of Chicago, not far from Wrigley Field, until 1952. When I was ten years old, our family moved to the suburbs, and I attended parochial school in Grades 1 to 8. I always liked the academic part of school but didn't care much for the social part. After I graduated from high school in 1960, I enrolled at a junior college (at my mother's insistence). Suddenly everything changed. For some inexplicable reason, the social aspects of college began to interest me, and I became part of a group of some fifteen people, about half of them men and half of them women. Some romantic involvements occurred in the group, and I discovered that women were very interesting!

Over the next couple of years, several of the people in our group decided to transfer to Southern Illinois University in Carbondale, Illinois. I eagerly joined them, and from 1963 to 1965, I worked toward my BA degree. During that time I dated various women but never experienced feelings of permanence in any of my relationships. But the social whirl was a great deal of fun, and university was an extremely positive experience for me.

One of my acquaintances at SIU was a woman who lived in an off-campus apartment with three other women. Many people gathered at their apartment on the weekends to socialize and play all-night card games. Pinochle (pronounced pea-knuckle) was the game of choice. People would drift in and out, and some would sit in on the games as needed.

In the first week of December 1965, I had completed my BA and was getting ready to leave Carbondale and move back home, where I would try to figure out what I should do in the next phase of my life. One evening that week, when I was playing cards at the apartment, one of the roommates I had never met came in from a date. She sat down at the table, and I was introduced to Ann. I immediately thought, "Hmmm, this could be interesting!" By the end of the evening, I had decided that I wanted to get to know her better. But because I was leaving town in a few days, and she was two years away from graduating, that was going to be a problem.

After thinking about this dilemma, I had a brilliant idea that would end up affecting both my personal and professional life: I would enroll in the MBA program in the spring of 1966. That way I could pretty well guarantee a good career, *and* I would be able to go out with Ann on a regular basis. This plan worked well. We dated, and soon fell in love. Before I met Ann, I had never given much thought to a long-term relationship with anyone, much less getting married, but now these thoughts were continually on my mind. Beause we were both in school, I didn't act on them right away, but in the spring of 1967, I said, "Let's get married."

Upon reflection, that was not a particularly romantic approach, but it was decisive. We were married in September 1967, and we celebrated fifty-five years of marriage in 2022.

I often reflect on the path that people's lives can take based on one decision, and how things might have been so different if they hadn't made that decision. If I had decided not to play cards that evening, I would never have met Ann. What would my life have been like without her? It's difficult to answer questions like these, but I am glad I was playing cards on that Friday evening, the first week in December, so many years ago.

LYNN LAKUSIAK

Lynn, a mother and grandmother, resides in Winnipeg. Gene, her husband of fifty-three years, played in the Canadian Football League for eight years and was later diagnosed with Alzheimer's. He passed away in July 2020 during the Covid pandemic lockdown. Lynn, a yoga practitioner and teacher for twenty-seven years, leaned into the nurturing and solace of her practice during Gene's illness, and continues to do so. Her story was written prior to Gene's passing.

The Look

I am standing with my girlfriend, Nancy, at the concession stand, holding my 5-cent banana Popsicle, basking in the sunny warmth of a 1965 July day. I have my back to Canatara Beach—the place to be for the young and the restless. It's a golden, sandy mecca on the shores of Lake Huron, where summer students gather to hang out. The beach is thronged with girls clad in bright polka-dotted bikinis and pastel gingham headscarves and guys in madras plaid jams topped with college insignia T-shirts. The scent of Coppertone wafts through the air. Transistor radios blare out a cacophony of top hits, including my favourites: "I (Can't Get No) Satisfaction," "I Can't Help Myself," and "Mr. Tambourine Man." I wriggle my toes into the sand in tentative anticipation of what to do next. Then, I feel it. In the midst of this sensory overload, I feel the magnetism of The Look. It draws me up and out of my shyness, giving me the momentum to turn around and eye the crowded beach. My gaze homes in on him. I see his athletic form way down the beach, standing midst a bevy of his buddies. He's staring directly at me. What happens next is unprecedented for me. I stride toward him, our blue eyes locked in on each other. I hand him half of my banana Popsicle then turn and walk away. This silent exchange of sweetness takes merely a moment. Tingling the whole way back to Nancy, I blurt out, "I can't believe what I just did."

***

Our silent and sweet exchange on that summer day was one of those synchronistic and mysteriously predestined moments in time. Both Gene and I were stirred to our very core. We followed our instincts, and what unfolded over the next two years laid the groundwork for a lifetime commitment to each other.

The common thread throughout the ups and downs of our married life has been The Look. It has grounded me when the roller coaster ride has gotten particularly crazy. That look that wordlessly conveys, "I'm happy to see you. I adore you. I'm here for you." I came to depend on it.

Then forty-some years after that life-altering look, it was in a yoga class that I noticed the change. He was a student, and I was the teacher.

He sat in the back, and when he raised his eyes to meet mine, I was met with a veiled vacancy. This new look numbed my whole being.

And then we were navigating a diagnosis of Alzheimer's that we believed to be a result of concussion trauma resulting from his years of playing football, both in university and professionally. It became a foggy and unpredictable path along which we groped from day to day. There were moments when The Look would return, and I would become hopeful. Even when he couldn't remember what happened two minutes earlier, he would occasionally look my way with a shy smile, and there it was—that recognizable spark in his still very blue eyes.

Could I nudge him out from under his cloud of confusion? Perhaps not. Could I pull him up with a look that's fueled from that same depth that started it all so many years ago. I certainly tried. Now it was my turn to convey to him wordlessly, "I'm here for you."

The story of The Look is the story I now tell myself to remind me of my 2.5-cent investment all those years ago.

ALICE HOGUE

Alice is from Winnipeg, but currently lives in Brandon, Manitoba, where she worked at Brandon University for twenty-seven years. Alice recalls the more than half century she spent with her first true love.

The Dance

I used to babysit for Aunt Sheila. She was the Director of the North YMCA on McGregor Street in Winnipeg, and she thought I should be able to enjoy the bands too, even when she had to be working at the

Y. So she hired another sitter for the kids one night and let me come with her.

And that's where I met Larry. I was sixteen and he was nineteen. We'd seen each other around the Y, and unknown to me, he'd been looking for a chance to talk to me. I had just started seeing another great fella—Rick—but he was teaching swimming at another Y in Winnipeg that night.

North YMCA hosted the Manitoba Battle of the Bands in Winnipeg, and Larry was a member of the Senior Leader Core at North Y—the organization that hired the bands. The band started playing their awesome music, and I was a standing wallflower, enjoying the music and watching others boogying on the dance floor. Suddenly, I felt someone tall beside me. I looked up and saw Larry. We smiled and said hello and introduced ourselves. He was funny and sooooo gooooooood looking—tall, dark, and handsome, with beautiful blue eyes. He told me he liked my smile from across the room. I smiled again. But all the time I was wondering, "What's with this guy? He knows I'm dating Rick."

Larry stood with me awhile, chatting about the band; the sold-out crowd was rocking to the music, and the gym walls were vibrating. He told me about some of the people in the Senior Core Group and about the Y. It was a comfortable feeling—like we had always known each other. Then he asked me to dance, and I said, "I don't think that would be a good idea. I just started seeing Rick."

"You'll have more fun with me," Larry said. "Let's dance."

So I danced with him. After all, how much could rock and roll affect us? We joined a group, and I had a blast. Then came a slow dance. My heart was pounding! Should I be doing this? Larry put his hands out, I took them, and we danced The Dance, closer and closer.

The rest is history. My First True Love danced his way into my heart and soul for fifty-two years. We dated for three years and were married for forty-nine. We fought and we made up. Marriage is a roller coaster, and we enjoyed the highs and rode out the lows. We have two wonderful sons, two lovely daughters-in-law, and four beautiful grandchildren. All from The Dance.

Aunt Sheila had known Larry as a member of the Senior Leader Core for many years, and she adored him. But never did she think I'd find my First True Love during The Dance at the North YMCA.

We lived. We loved. We laughed. We cried. Then Larry slowly danced away from me. Sadly, October 23, 2016, he died of liver disease.

SHIRLEY YOUNKIN

Shirley is a former math teacher, the VP of a small business, and a native plant devotee who has volunteered for over twenty years at her local arboretum, maintaining the Woodland Wildflower Garden. She and Dave have been married for fifty-three years; they have two children.

Shirley has written another story that appears in the "Not All Love is Romantic" section of this book. Because I couldn't bear to part with either of them, here is her story about her first true love, romantic style.

Close Encounters of the Noisy Kind

For a couple of months, my roommate and I had put up with the noise but had never encountered the neighbour in the apartment downstairs, resorting to turning our Fisher XP66 speakers to face the floor in hopes of counteracting his stereo.

And then one evening, while we were hosting a sorority after-party, he showed up at our door to complain about our noise level, telling us that he had to get up early to go on a trip. Of all the nerve! But he was kinda cute.

On a sarcastic impulse, we left a note on his door: "Sorry about the noise—hope you have a good trip—C1."

Next morning, there's a note on our door: "If you're sorry about the noise, you'll invite me up for a drink when I get back—B1."

Followed by a note on his door: "Why not?"

The drinks go well, he's smart and very nice. (And did I say cute?) So for a month or so, the three of us hung out. FINALLY, my roommate went home for the weekend, and he asked me out to dinner. It was perfect—good food and great conversation. Back at the apartment, good music (not so noisy now) and great conversation. And then that first kiss—MAGIC!!!

And after fifty years, it still is.

NAN HAYMAN

Nan lives in Kelowna BC with her first true love. She's a mother of two, an avid sewer, and a woman of many hats: office administrator, homemaker, mother, grandmother, and volunteer, to name a few. Nan loves sunshine, lakes, and new adventures. And she's continuing to work on her passion: travelling to other countries.

Chance Encounters

I attended Victoria High School for Grades 11 and 12. In Grade 11, I took a math class that I despised. My reaction was to walk in with my head down, sit at my desk, and wait for the class to end.

One day another girl in the math class asked me if I had seen the guy who sat behind me. "His name is Bill. He's so handsome," she said. "And he plays soccer and rugby for the school."

Hmm—maybe I should take a look. Yep—definitely good looking and definitely an athlete. Now what?

A week later, I was heading downtown to do some Christmas shopping. As I got off the bus, Bill walked by the bus stop. He stopped to talk to me, and we went for coffee. And the rest, as they say, is history.

We met in December 1978, went to college and university together, married in July 1985, and have two children and a grandchild. We recently celebrated our thirty-fifth wedding anniversary by traveling to Europe for six weeks. Our life is filled with laughter and adventures.

Oh, and for the record: The girl in my math class never spoke to me again after she learned that Bill and I were dating.

JÓN BJARMAN

I wish that my dear friends Jón Bjarman and Hanna Pálsdóttir could have read this book, but they both passed away before that was possible. Jón was a pastor and author, who spent much of his career working with youth groups and working with and advocating for prisoners around the world. Hanna was a banking executive turned painter who soon became famous around Iceland and beyond in her second career as a visual artist. Hanna and Jón were born less than a month apart; they fell in love at sixteen, married at twenty-one, and spent the next fifty-seven years together in Canada, USA, and Iceland.

The following story is an excerpt from Jón's book, *Af Föngum og Frjálsum Mönnum* (*Of Free Men and Jailed*), translated by Ármann Ingólfsson, and reprinted here in English with the kind permission of Hanna and the Icelandic publishing house, Bókaútgáfan Hólar.

Falling in Love with an Angel

I think it was in March 1949 that assembly was called, as often happened in Menntaskólinn á Akureyri [Akureyri Junior College]. I hurried upstairs to the residences in the north end of the building and pushed my way into the group that was gathered around the piano because I expected that the headmaster would let us sing. I glanced diagonally across the room and saw a girl that I had not noticed before. She was rather tall, slim, very fair, and had long, blonde hair, which was gathered together at the back of her head through some mysterious means.

After assembly, I began to inquire about this girl because I was transported to seventh heaven. I was told that her name was Jóhanna Katrín, that she was the daughter of a pastor from Öxarfjörður, and that she wrote her name Hanna Pálsdóttir.

I spoke to two of my friends and told them that I had seen my future wife, a girl who was more like an angel than a human.

And she became my wife.

* * *

NOTE FROM NINA: Life wasn't always a bed of roses for Jón and Hanna, of course, especially after Jón was diagnosed with Parkinson's Disease. But again, love prevailed, reminding me of Ursula LeGuin's famous quote: "Love doesn't just sit there, like a stone; it has to be made, like bread, remade all the time, made new." Again, I draw on Ármann's translation of Jón's autobiography.

* * *

Hanna…has not shown me pity, but has treated me the same as before, made the same demands of me, and never viewed me as a patient. Nevertheless she is considerate of me, stands by my side, and follows me in joy and sorrow.

KRISTÍN AÐALSTEINSDÓTTIR

Kristín has retired from her career as a professor at the University of Akureyri, but she still enjoys interviewing people and listening to their stories. Over the past five years, she has published five books based on her interviews and illustrated with her photographs of people.

In the next two stories, Kristín and her husband Hallgrímur offer us new perspectives on first love—the perspectives of two people who have spent over half a century together.

Him

The summer I turned eighteen, I worked in Akureyri—a small town in Northern Iceland—as a domestic helper for a married couple with two grown-up sons. I had been in the home for a few days when I heard that the sons were planning a trip to the mountains with their friends the following Saturday, taking two cars. I had never been on such a trip and asked if I could go with them. "No, it's not possible." I was told that there

My First *True* Love

was no room in the cars. I had nothing to say in the matter, so I had to be content with that answer.

The following Friday, when I was cleaning the house, dressed like any other housemaid (on top of which, I had curlers in my hair—after all, this was 1964), there was a knock on the door. I opened it, and a young man I had never seen before was standing on the doorstep—tall and handsome, in a tan suede jacket, looking confident. He greeted me and told me he had heard that I wanted to join the trip to the mountain of Askja. He went on to say that he had been there many times and would be happy for me to take his seat in one of the cars. I thanked him warmly and accepted the offer. It never occurred to me not to.

The Saturday of the mountain journey arrived, and it was time to go. By then the handsome boy had managed to obtain a third car for the journey. (He was also clever.) I was then able to have a place in this car with him and his two friends, who turned out to be quiet types who didn't say much. I got to sit up front between the driver and the handsome boy, and we started talking. We hadn't sat side by side in the car for long when I remember thinking, "What fun, and what a handsome boy!"

On the way back to Akureyri, I felt asleep, and when I woke up, his arm was around my shoulders. I remember it as if it had happened yesterday. It was love at first sight. I was eighteen years old, and he was almost seventeen. We have been married for over fifty years and have three children and four grandchildren. Although I have always found him handsome, it was Hallgrímur's thoughtfulness I fell for. He has always been the same.

* * *

HALLGRÍMUR INDRIÐASON

Hallgrímur is a poet who turned his love of the outdoors and his teenage job working at a tree nursery in Akureyri into a career as a forester. Here Hallgrímur refocuses the prism to tell us the other side of the Kristín–Hallgrímur story.

Her

In the spring of 1964, I had temporarily taken a job at a plant nursery in the forest in Akureyri, as I had done for a few previous years. I had no specific thoughts about my future. I loved being part of the Scouts and travelling around the country with my friends. I didn't really want to be tied down by work if it interfered with possible adventures with a tent and a rucksack.

Mid-May that same year I had gone on a graduation trip with my schoolmates to South Iceland and stopped by in Reykjavík for the first time in my life. My travelling companions were boys and girls I had known since before I started school. In this trip a few relationships started, which still remain.

But I had other plans. I had planned to take a trip with good friends to Herðubreiðarlindir and Askja and to prepare the hut owned by the Akureyri Hiking Club located in the area. We also intended to mark some trails.

When I came back to my hometown of Akureyri, I heard that a Girl Scout from Kópavogur had arrived in town and was planning to work as a domestic helper in the home of people I knew from my neighbourhood. She was also planning to work part time at the nursery in the forest. This was indeed interesting news in a small town like Akureyri.

I was told that she was interested in joining our trip to the highlands to Askja, that she was ready to lend a hand in clearing up and cleaning the mountain hut, but that there was no room for an extra person in the car. This problem resulted in my going to introduce myself to the new girl and offering her my seat in the car. I knew that no one would come back unchanged from a trip to Askja or the old volcano, Herðubreið, and I wanted her to experience that. The girl, who said her name was Kristín, was happy to accept my offer and quick to get ready for the trip.

In the meantime, I successfully managed to find another car that was well equipped for mountain trips, and another seat became available. As chance would have it, Kristín and I travelled in the same car. I was the only person in the group that Kristín had ever talked to before, and we had many things to talk about. I liked her. In Askja we drove around lava and rocky trails, and it could be said that Kristín and I were shaken together after travelling those bumpy mountain trails for 300 kilometres.

That summer we became sweethearts, although no mutual demands were made. We shared an interest in hiking and were always able to laugh and discuss things together and to have a good time with our friends.

This trip was the beginning of an adventure that has lasted for over fifty years. We have often been apart because of the demands of jobs or studies, but that has only had a positive effect on our relationship.

I'm planning on taking her to Askja again as soon as possible.

BRENT PATTERSON

Brent and his wife, Marie-Josée, provide us with a second twinned story of first true love. Brent (aka Babe) has spent thirty years in the banking and the hedge fund industries. Currently living in Montreal with Marie-Josée and their three boys, his career has taken them to multiple locations in Canada, USA, and Asia. When Brent is not working or spending time with his family, he feeds his passion of watching Formula One racing or driving his sports car or motorbike in the mountains around the family's country chalet just north of Montreal.

Love at First Sight

My first true love is more about love at first sight than it is about first true love. The two aren't necessarily mutually inclusive, but in my case they are—absolutely. Finding one's true love at first sight is a truly fantastic experience, and this is my story.

I saw Marie-Josée from afar for the first time in 1987, and the feeling that came over me—mind and body—was overwhelming. I had laid eyes on the person that I wanted to spend the rest of my life with. Not a conscious feeling, but a feeling that this person and I need to be together forever—my other half—so now I could be whole.

It's thirty-plus years later, and we're married with three wonderful boys and still living in complete harmony. People who know what it is like to find the other person who makes them whole are as lucky as I am.

I have love, respect, and admiration for this truly talented mother, role model, and pivotal centre of our universe. She is loved by everyone who meets her, but we are lucky to call her our own.

It makes me proud when our boys say they can see the love between their parents, as it has been that way since my first sight of my first true love.

My first true love happens to be my only true love—a force that provides my balance, drive, and life. If I knew why or could explain it, I would. But I can't. A bond formed at first sight, sculpted over time, continuously strengthening and changing as we grow old together. My first true love is my only true love and my last true love!

Love you, Babe. xx

***

MARIE-JOSÉE PAQUET

And now for the second half of the Brent–Marie-Josée story.

When I asked Marie-Josée to write me a biographical sketch, she gave me this wonderful response:

> Young college girl who was swept away by love? Innocent country girl? Fulfilled middle-aged woman? Woman with a positive attitude and focused mindset, professionally speaking? Caregiver who wants to give everything to her mother? Friend who loves to entertain and thrives on organizing and planning social gatherings? Cool Maman?

Babe: What's in a Name?

I remember when I first started dating Brent as if it were yesterday. I remember the feeling of being loved, of having someone in love with me. I felt like I was the only one in the world for him. I still feel like that today, some thirty years later. I remember his shouting from his car window to my car, next to him, "I love you." I remember not being able to answer back. I wasn't sure if I was in love with him. I wanted to tell him I was, but I also wanted to be sure of my love before I declared it.

What is love? What is true love? At first it's having butterflies every time you see him and jitters every time he touches you. It's missing classes just to stay in his arms for a few more minutes. This is falling in love. As you age together, build a family, build memories, go through rough and good times, the meaning of love changes. He is the love of my life. When he isn't with me in the evening, I miss him like a part of me is missing. As we take our walks together, we exchange, debate, reminisce.

He's my best friend. He's the man I love. He's my complement. He is my only love.

Lost Loves

> I only know that summer sang in me
> a little while,
> that in me sings no more.
>
> - Edna St. Vincent Millay

Ever since Shakespeare wrote about the ill-fated Romeo and Juliet, and probably long before, stories about lost love have touched the hearts and excited the imaginations of writers and readers, storytellers and listeners. The happiest of these stories end in re-found love—in the couple reuniting and forming an even stronger bond. The saddest end, as Shakespeare has told us, is when "A pair of star-cross'd lovers take their life." And somewhere in between are most of the stories: the couples that separate, go their own ways, and may or may not find new loves.

I was particularly taken by a story about Norwood Thomas and Joyce Morris, separated, as *The Washington Post* relayed, "by WWII, 70 years and 10,000 miles." They had met in London during the war, and after he proposed and was refused, they lost track of each other. Joyce moved to Australia, Norwood moved to USA, and they married other people and raised families. But they often asked themselves, "What if?"

And then Joyce, who was divorced, asked her son to try to find Thomas, who, it turned out, was a widower. And in 2015, after they had found each other again, *The Virginian-Pilot* wrote a story about them, Air New Zealand picked up the story and presented Thomas with a flight to visit Joyce, and they were reunited once again.

Joyce and Thomas have since died, but their love story has warmed the hearts of millions who saw the videos and read the stories. And if you enter "Norwood Thomas and Joyce Morrison" into your search engine, their story can warm your heart as well.

In the meantime, here are six completely different but equally poignant stories about lost loves.

A STORYTELLER FROM PALERMO

A Lost Hand

My first true love was Rossana. I still remember her eyes, her intense gaze. But I was too shy in primary school to declare my love. Once she took my hand, and I ran away. I lost the opportunity to become a young man. I saw her again at the university for a few moments, although I wasn't sure it was her. From time to time I happen to see a woman who looks the way she would possibly look now, and I wonder how it might have been if I had held her hand.

GWEN KALANSKY

Gwen is a retired family physician, living in Gimli, Manitoba, with her second love.

Thank You, Nick

Nick and I met in September 1964 at a Hootenanny that the Anglican Young Peoples' Association had organized at my church. Nick had come from the North End of Winnipeg with two of his friends, Art and Zbig. I remember that I had borrowed a friend's black dress to wear for the occasion. Nick asked me to dance, and he later told me that he had looked across the room, admired my beautiful legs, and just had to meet me. He was tall and handsome and muscular, with beautiful blue eyes. He was seventeen and I was sixteen.

Just before I met Nick, I had had a baby and had given her up for adoption, so I was in a highly traumatized state and loved his kind, caring manner. He stayed the whole evening, helped my friends and me clean up, and then walked me home. Zbig and Art had already left, so Nick ended up having to take a bus home.

Mum and Dad were up waiting for me. I remember Dad peering over his newspaper at Nick, immediately asking him where he was from and what he was doing. But Nick and my parents eventually became best of friends. They called him their son and he called them Mum and Dad.

Nick and I started dating regularly after that first meeting—going to movies, walking, and talking. Through our first forays of getting to know each other, we shared our hopes, dreams, and pasts. I learned that

Nick lived with his dad in a boarding house in the North End. His dad worked as a labourer for the City of Winnipeg. He was an alcoholic. His mother, who was also an alcoholic, left them when Nick was just three years old.

The most important person in Nick's life was his grandmother. Granny bought him shoes when he had none, encouraged him to do his best in everything he tried, and fed him good Ukrainian food, which was very different from the boarding house grab-and-eat fare. She supported him through his darkest times as a toddler; a teen; and an aspiring athlete in hockey, soccer, and baseball. She became a shining example of love and kindness in my life as well and in the lives of our children. They likely remember the special cookies in the blue tin that Granny always had for them when we visited her in Lion's Manor, where she moved after she'd lived with us for a few months. Granny died at the age of one hundred and two, with Nick at her side.

I remember one time when Nick took me to a movie, and we stopped at The Chocolate Shop Restaurant after the show. I ordered a sundae, and when he took me home, he was embarrassed that he didn't have enough money for bus fare to get home—he had spent it all on the movie and the sundae for me. In those days, guys always paid for everything on a date. But he had asked me to lend him money for bus fare to get home. Humility was yet another one of Nick's beautiful qualities.

At one point, I suggested to Nick that he should be more assertive, and even went so far to break up with him to give him time to think about it. A few months after our separation, he told Art and Zbig that he was going to ask me out one more time, and that if I didn't say "yes," he would give up. I was so thankful that I immediately said "yes." Did he become more assertive? Yes. But to that end, he brought his skills of patience, of course. And by then, I had had time to reflect on his many qualities and to realize that I had fallen in love.

In spite of his dad's alcohol problem, Nick never displayed anger toward him or told me that he felt angry at him, and he never gave up on him. Nor did I. We even had him come to live with us in our apartment for a while after he was discharged from the hospital. He eventually died from hemorrhaging, alcohol-related esophageal varices in the McLaren Hotel, where he had been living for many years. Nick held no anger towards his mother either. He made sure I met her and her husband—both alcoholics—in Calgary. Years later Nick flew to Calgary to be at her side when she was dying.

At one point in his many careers, Nick was the CEO of a large organization. He cared about his co-workers and their families and knew all their names and their stories as genuine people—not just as employees. Everyone loved him.

Nick was the kindest, most tolerant, understanding, humble, supportive person I have ever known. He cared about everyone, no matter who they were or what they had done.

The happiest day of my life was the day I married my first true love at twenty-two. And the saddest and most horrific day of my life was the day he died at fifty. Our ups and downs were legion, as with all couples, but there were many wonderful memories, like travelling in Europe for a year in our VW camper. (During that time I began talking about applying for medical school. His answer, with no hesitation, was, "Go for it!") Then there was the joy of the births and maturing of our two precious children and our successes in both our chosen careers—just a few of my many special memories. We had many plans for our future: travelling after retirement, revelling in our children's successes, enjoying grandchildren....

But his death was sudden and unexpected, giving us no chance to prepare for the devastating loss.

Nick's example and teaching have made me a kinder, more patient, supportive, and tolerant person, enabling me to go on and love again.

Thank you, Nick. My First True Love.

GERALDINE GILMOUR

Geraldine describes herself as a retired teacher, musician, and author.

Never Forgotten

Throughout my ninety-plus years on earth, I have experienced great surges of love for family members (including four amazing brothers, my two children, and three grandchildren); for places (Budapest, CAMMAC Music Centre in the Laurentians, the Grand Canyon, and all of New England); for orchestral music (the first time I heard the slow movement of Mahler's 5th Symphony, I thought I'd died and gone to heaven); and finally, for my favourite music maker—a Heintzman upright piano I purchased at the age of twenty-one, shortly after I embarked on a career as a practising musician in Saint John, New Brunswick. I found this piano in a local music shop and was captivated by it from the moment I ran my fingers over the keyboard. Scarlatti, Bach, and Paradies never sounded so satisfying; some pianos almost play themselves, and this was one of them. It saw me through most of my musical growth and gave me no end of joy. Was I in love with that piano? You bet your boots!

But what of my first romantic love? I've had a few nibbles at "head over heels" encounters with members of the opposite sex from childhood onward. Out-of-reach idols included Flash Gordon (a comic book adventurer) and Errol Flynn (a handsome movie Lothario). When I was seven years old and living in Fredericton, NB, I was badly smitten with a twelve-year-old lad who cycled by our home each morning on his way to school. I can't remember what he looked like, but I'll never forget the way I felt when I caught a glimpse of him. He probably didn't even know I existed.

My adolescent years were peppered with shy advances from young suitors I met in high school. A few sparks were ignited at sports and social events, house parties and dances, mostly in group situations. I was attracted to William, a Jason Robards Jr. look-alike and a classmate who took me to our graduation dance. We were considered a couple until our paths diverged; I moved to Montreal to attend university and William remained in New Brunswick, where he worked for an oil company, married, and raised a family. After we parted as teenagers, we made a few stabs at corresponding, but our romance eventually fizzled out.

Surprisingly, after a hiatus of thirty years, William re-entered my life. He appeared on my doorstep in Brandon (I had moved to the Prairies in 1969) while on a trip across the country to connect with former classmates and friends. He was retired, recently divorced, and anxious to pick up some threads from our past. We decided to take several road trips together and became good travel companions. The sparks of our teenaged romance were never reignited, however, and we parted as good friends. After we lost touch, I learned that he remarried, this time to a woman who brought him happiness and nursed him through his final illness over a decade ago.

Donald Roy was another matter. I met him at a summer resort hotel in Tadoussac, Quebec, when I was nineteen and Donald was twenty-two. The hotel hired university students each summer to fill jobs in the hospitality industry. Donald was studying pre-med at McGill; I was a music student. I served as a waitress and played classical music for guests in the evenings. Donald bussed tables and conducted the dance band three times a week. Many friendships amongst staff were forged throughout the two summers we worked there. First dates often led to coupling, some resulting in marriage. What drew Donald and me together following our first date was our common interest in music, especially jazz. He coached me through a variety of keyboard styles and helped me to change my improvisational approach. He taught me to use cluster chords à la Errol Garner and to distinguish among stride piano, be-bop, swing, and ragtime. I play the way I do today because of Donald.

Our relationship deepened and continued to grow beyond the time we spent together in Tadoussac. We lived within blocks of each other in Outremont and saw each other regularly over a two-year courtship. We went to dances, sports events, movies, and ball games, played in the same dance band combos, and even studied together. We fell in love and spoke of marriage and family life. Donald had chosen the ring.

All went well, until my father visited Montreal, met Donald, and learned that he was a practising Roman Catholic. (I had been brought up as a member of the United Church of Canada.) On a school break, when I returned to my Campbellton home, I found a number of tracts in my bedroom that featured such titles as *Why Mixed Marriages Don't Work*, *If I Marry Roman Catholic*, and *What Will Happen to my Children?* I knew my father would confront me to discuss these issues. He told me that I was flirting with the pope and that my mother would be rolling over in her grave. He wanted to know how I felt about bringing up my children in the Catholic faith, to which I responded, "I'd be happy if they turned out to be as fine and honourable as their father."

But at my father's insistence, I broke my engagement to Donald and returned to an emptier, lonelier world in Montreal. In the Campbellton of the 1950s, the English didn't mate with the French, Blacks didn't marry Whites, and Irish Catholics rarely fraternized with French Catholics. High schools were segregated. My mother's brother, Alphonse, refused to attend her marriage ceremony when she wed my father (a Scottish Protestant who attended the same church as she did as a French Protestant). That's the way it was.

Because of the proximity of our homes, Donald and I were bound to meet on buses or on campus after we broke up. We ran into each other on a bus one night and sat together for five stops, speaking only briefly before I disembarked. It was a poignant few minutes, after which we waved to each other from opposite sides of the window, shades of *Dr. Zhivago*. Shortly after that parting in 1950, I moved to Saint John, met other men (to one of whom I became engaged—the engagement didn't last) and met a man my father approved of. A friend sent a news clipping accompanied by a photo of Donald's engagement to a fellow Catholic in Montreal. He was now a well-established dentist.

I married within ten months of meeting Jeremy and gave birth to a daughter, then a son. The marriage foundered and didn't last. When we parted in 1959, I settled in Southern New Brunswick, where I worked as a school music teacher for nine years before moving to a position at a post-secondary institution.

In the early 1980s, my daughter, now an established music teacher in Montreal, made a dental appointment with a Dr. Donald Roy, who practised near her home. When they met and conversed and she told him who her mother was, he exclaimed, "I could have been your father!" They arranged for a reunion on one of my overnight stopovers en route home from Florida. He was scheduled to play with his orchestra on the night of my visit and suggested that I attend with my daughter. I remember that I was dressed in mauve and hoped he would remember me. He did. We were able to reminisce during the band's breaks with the conversation revolving around our continued involvement in the musical world. We enjoyed the encounter and parted amicably. I knew that he was a successful dentist and had raised a family of six.

When another twenty-five years had elapsed, my daughter sent me a news clipping announcing Donald's death. He had married twice and had been living in a personal care home. I hoped he hadn't died alone, for no mention was made of his wives. When I read the obituary, I sat at my piano and played his arrangements of "I'll Close My Eyes" and "We'll Be Together Again."

There have been other loves in my life—happy times spent with male companions who were supportive and caring. Yet I never felt about them the way I felt about Donald.

Writing about one's first love implies that there may have been a second or third meaningful romantic relationship. Yet I've heard it said that to have such a love reciprocated once in a lifetime is one of life's richest blessings. I have had that bestowal. The twelve-year-old lad who tugged at my heart strings when I was seven years old was simply an eye blink, a passing fancy. I consider Donald to have been not only my first, but also my last true love.

CONNI CARTLIDGE

Conni raised her family on the banks of Wavey Creek in Manitoba's Interlake. A retired college instructor, she now helps care for her mother and her grandchildren. Her stories and poems reflect her love for these people and places. Thank you, Conni, for allowing me to adapt this story about Mary and Andrew from your blog:

http://conni-smallboxes.blogspot.com

And thank you, Mary for allowing your story to be told.

Percentages

0% chance of cure means manicures right?
#icebergrightahead #fuckcancer

That was the Facebook status I read. That was how I learned that my daughter's first love was not going to make it.

Mary met Andrew at nursery school. It was not love at first sight. He was a confident four-year-old senior, and she was a timid junior, only three at the time. She sat at the Playdough table watching the other children, too shy to join in.

When both children graduated to kindergarten, Mary attended a small community school. Andrew bravely took the bus to the French-immersion school in a nearby city. For many years, they lost touch, even though they lived only 4 kilometres apart.

Everything changed in high school when their love of the arts reunited them. All grades played and worked together on drama productions and symphonic concerts. Andrew's seniority no longer mattered, and Mary was beginning to find her own voice. He drove her home after late night rehearsals of *The Crucible*. They laughed together in the back row of the school band as they kept the beat in the percussion section. She finally announced to me that they were "going out." Andrew was her first boyfriend. She was sixteen. She was head over heels.

When he started coming around our house on a regular basis, I was happy for both of them. They giggled. They made silly videos, always including Mary's little brother. They hosted parties for their group of self-proclaimed band-geek and drama-nerd friends. On Hallowe'en, everyone wore costumes. Mary was a rag doll and Andrew was a ghost. They played hide and seek outside in the dark, screaming and squealing and stealing kisses, I'm sure.

Andrew charmed Mary's grandparents by attending family dinners. His ability to chat with anyone put us at ease. And he treated Mary like a queen. They got all dressed up to attend symphonies and plays, she in her vintage black cocktail dress and he in a sharp suit, both beaming from ear to ear.

But over time, some distance developed. Andrew moved into his own apartment, while Mary was still finishing high school. One afternoon as I was packing to go away for a few days, Mary came out of her room in tears. "Andrew broke up with me," she sobbed. "I don't know why."

I held her as she cried and cried and cried. And I was cursing him in my head, knowing that I had a plane to catch and couldn't stay long with Mary. She assured me she would be okay and that she would get together with her best friend while I was gone. We talked on the phone several times a day, and when I returned, she seemed to have accepted the situation. I was probably angry longer than she. How dare he break my daughter's heart?

Some time later, Andrew moved to Toronto. Mary went to his going-away party, and I marvelled at her open-mindedness. I was still holding a bit of a grudge.

The going away became Andrew's coming out.

Freed from small-town Manitoba, Andrew found his true self. My daughter's first boyfriend became her best gay boyfriend. Suddenly, it all made sense.

When she moved to Toronto a year later, Andrew was there for her. He took her to Nuit Blanche, and they recorded a tangled video of themselves wrapped in string, laughing hysterically in the middle of the night. They posted YouTube videos, with Andrew giving garish make-up lessons to Mary. As I watched their antics from afar, I felt relieved that Mary had a hometown friend with her in the big city. He was an anchor for her. He was a comfort for me. It was a new kind of love.

And now, Andrew has cancer.

It is terminal.

He is twenty-seven years old.

Mary phoned me last night. She was crying again. She had said her final good-byes to Andrew at a "funeral dance party" in Toronto. At the end of the night, Andrew said to Mary's friend, "Take good care of my Mary."

Andrew is headed back to Manitoba with his mother. He is coming home to die. He has planned his funeral. He wants glamour, glitter, Madonna, and Cher. I know I will fly Mary home for this.

100% chance she will always love him.

***

Andrew is coming over to watch the Oscars with me tomorrow night if he's able. I will give him a copy of the story then. I want him to know how much he means to all of us. Before he is gone.

***

Mary flew home from Toronto and attended Andrew's funeral yesterday in Clandeboye. She was able to say a tearful farewell to him and keep a red rose from his casket. The love has not died. Never will.

WYNNE

Wynne prefers to remain anonymous.

None Could Compare

He was the first one I ever fully trusted. He was certainly the first one I confided in, to the depth that I did. He knew everything about me and loved me anyway. I can honestly say he loved me unconditionally. Knowing that, I loved him passionately and unreservedly.

He was in my life for only two years, but in that brief time I enjoyed a level of companionship and trust that I didn't experience again for many years, perhaps never have, exactly. I suppose my youth and innocence lent to a purity of love that was yet untarnished by the reality that we are sometimes disillusioned even by those we love deeply.

I remember vividly the day he walked into my life. The thrill was unparalleled that first time he came across the room toward me. I don't know if I knew before that moment that it was possible to have such energy race through my body and swell in my heart. I remember the excitement still.

I was young. Too young for that relationship to last. Yet, somehow, no one has ever come close to filling that spot in my heart all these years later. None could compare.

I suppose at first, I thought he was cute. In time I came to appreciate how handsome he really was, even if others didn't see it. But then, I had a relationship with him that no one else had. I saw his beauty deep beneath the surface. I was the recipient of his immense intuition and deep compassion.

My father was fond of him. I have wondered if Dad confided in him. It's possible. He was an ideal confidant.

They spent time together, he and Dad, and they got along well, but I considered him wholly mine.

He had the most gorgeous brown eyes. They looked deep into mine with an understanding no one had before or has since. It was like he could see deep inside me to places I hadn't yet seen.

One day, when Dad and I were working in the garden, he was there with us. I stepped with bare feet onto an old nail buried in the soil. I cried out in pain, and he was right there. As I sat on the patio quietly sniffling, while Mum tended to my wounded foot, he snuggled close, and I knew he felt my pain.

I don't believe I understood what a treasure I had until he was gone. I'm afraid I took it for granted that he would always be there for me. It hadn't occurred to me that it could be any different.

But one day I came home expecting to find him there as usual and asked my mother where he was. She told me about the accident, and said, "Don't mention it to your father. He's too upset." Years later I realized how those words prevented me from sharing with Dad something of the pain that filled both our hearts. Just as we shared his companionship, we could have shared our sorrow over his untimely death. Instead, we grieved alone.

Twelve years later, the man I was dating told me that he felt I was pushing him away—that I wouldn't let him get "too close." One day shortly after, I had a flashback, and I remembered my mother saying years earlier, "No, we won't get another pet. Something always happens to them." I realized in that moment I had translated that message into "It is not safe to love. Something may happen to disappoint and hurt." I recalled having said to Mum at the time, "No, another dog won't *replace* Alrae, but we can still love another."

Perhaps I had internalized her words more than I realized.

Recognition and revelation of thought are wonderful tools in healing, though. No, no dog could have ever replaced Alrae, but there have been other dogs I have loved keenly too. Each had its own loveable, beautiful ways. Some have been in my life for only moments, yet I can give you the details of those encounters.

Several years ago, at a large gathering of people from different areas, a woman greeted me by name. I said hello, but by the look on my face she knew I was going through the files in my mind, trying to remember who she was and where I had met her.

She quickly said, "You don't remember me, do you?"

"Well, I know I should, but I am sorry. I just can't place you."

With an understanding smile, she said, "I have the Labradoodle."

I knew instantly who she was and where I had met her in passing a couple of years before. But mostly I remembered meeting her gorgeous dog, my first encounter with that enchanting breed. I have laughed about that experience many times over the years, realizing I may not place people immediately, but I will remember their dogs. Yet now as I think back to my first true love, I understand that he set the bar for my canine friends.

No, no one has replaced him. No one could replace him. But there are others I have loved.

Lost Loves

JAY WILLIAMS

Jay is a retired lawyer living in an undisclosed location in the United States.

What's Love Got to Do With the BuRec?

(with apologies to Tina Turner)

The United States Bureau of Reclamation (BuRec) is an odd entity stuck in time between the 1930s depression and climate change. BuRec hired me in 1979 to work on a lake project in South Dakota (state name changed to protect the innocent). Apparently I was the only applicant with Hydrolab experience. A Hydrolab is something the operator lowers into the water to detect things like salinity, conductivity, pH, and whether there's life on other planets like South Dakota.

I embellished my Hydrolab experience, which may technically be a federal offence. But I was upfront about my Secchi disk experience. A Secchi disk is a white and black plate that's lowered into the water to determine the amount of algae or pollutants present. When it can't be seen anymore, the results are to be written down with a pencil. Always a pencil. Anyway, I got the job, and in the bargain I got a companion biologist who reminded me of the female lead in a 1930's movie starring twice-married Dutch Reagan. Reagan would not have approved of the relationship, but it's 2022 of this writing, and thrice-married Trump has already pardoned me along with half the other criminals of my ilk.

BuRec sent me and my now-companion of Scandinavian descent out together in a pickup truck to sample water in numerous lakes and streams and generally perform biologist-type duties. Biology ensued. We were in our early twenties. Our *per diem* payments provided unspendable largess in the countryside. We visited bars like drunken sailors a thousand miles from any ocean.

She considered herself a pool shark. Our first game of eight-ball resulted in my running the table after her sloppy break. It got her attention. We stayed in motels in separate rooms until that seemed like a futile gesture and a waste of government money. Nobody questioned the motel cohabitation impropriety. Budgets are budgets.

One time she made me take a compass into a phragmites marsh.

"Don't be silly. I'm only going in 30 metres or so." (I'm American, so I didn't really say that because even though we were biologists, we didn't talk in metres. I probably said 100 feet.)

I got lost. I'd still be decomposing away at the bottom of that marsh if she hadn't been there.

She hurt her knee playing that great American rural sport of softball. I had told her not to. But I nursed her back to health in a series of swimming pools dotting the landscape of wherever we were in rural America.

When the summer ended, she went back to Colorado (state name changed to protect the, by this point, no longer innocent) and grad school and her boyfriend. She got a PhD, even though she couldn't spell. She later ended up in a bikini, on a yacht somewhere warm with a professor from her doctoral thesis committee. Twenty-five years later I found her after reading about her husband on some online site that detailed his death in a plane crash. I got her a lawyer who didn't take half her money, and she lived happily ever after.

Last I heard anyway.

LARRY DENCHUK

Larry worked as a letter carrier for Canada Post for thirty-four years. He describes himself as having a characteristic that amazes many people: He has "been blessed/cursed" with an exceptional memory stored in a video file in his brain. As he plays one of these videos, he explains, he can look around and see what people are wearing and hear what they are saying. He says that "the best part of it is remembering all the stupid things I've done. It keeps me humble." Fortunately for us readers, Larry's memory has provided a highly detailed account of life before he turned seven.

Grandma's House

I don't think I ever truly understood what the word "love" meant for the first forty years of my life. It's not a word that was ever used in my childhood toward me or anyone else in my family circle. It was a TV word, used a lot it seemed, but not by real-life people.

I was born in Winnipeg in 1951, and from the age of three till almost seven, I lived with my parents and my sister, Linda, at my grandmother's house. It was my grandfather's too, but almost everyone referred to it as simply as "Grandma's House."

Grandma was an intelligent but uneducated cleaning lady, who could barely read. She cleaned house for a Winnipeg lawyer—Mr. Parker as she always referred to him—once or twice a week during the day. Five nights a week she cleaned a bank on Main and Dufferin that she reached by bus from the suburbs, often with me in tow, along with a shopping bag containing everything from cleaning supplies to an egg salad sandwich for us to share later. Grandma went nowhere without a full shopping bag! After cleaning the bank, we would take a bus out to St. James to clean a large, two-storey building that sold pianos. My job was emptying the metal garbage cans at each desk. I would be amazed at all the once-used carbon paper, or tracing paper as I called it, thrown out every day at the bank. If I could find a sheet that wasn't too crinkled, Grandma would let me take it home, and I'd trace all kinds of pictures and labels around the house. My aunts and my grandfather would tell me how absolutely amazing my "art" was and how smart and special I was.

Grandma was one of the most important people in my life. What she accomplished with just hard work and determination was remarkable. Her solution to all problems was, "Just work harder."

On Saturdays, Grandma didn't go to work, and if I was lucky enough to have my parents out for the evening and her babysitting, it would be the best night ever. We both loved to watch wrestling. Even better than that, she enjoyed making homemade donuts. I'll never forget the first time I saw her put raw dough into hot grease in the deep fryer for a few minutes; later, she turned each one over, and, like magic, there was a golden-brown donut, hole and all—the greatest thing I had ever seen in my short life. While they were cooling on newspaper to soak up the grease, she would sift icing sugar over them, and we would take a plate of them, still warm, into the living room, sit side by side, and watch wrestling and eat donuts. This is one of the best memories.

My life in this house, I realized much later, was my first real love. I loved living there. It was a brand new, three-bedroom, one-bathroom, 950-square-foot house in a new subdivision, far from our old place in the North End of Winnipeg near Main Street. To say we stood out from the rest of the community is an understatement. This is where young families lived with a husband, wife, and two or three children. We, on the other hand, consisted of a group of nine: my grandmother and grandfather; my three aunts, Edna, Lily, and Gladys; Mum and Dad; my sister, Linda; and me. I slept in a bedroom with three beds. Aunts Lily and Gladys had single beds, and my sister and I were in a double bed with Aunt Edna, my favourite aunt. As I think about that now, I find it hard to believe. We were a weird family, but I didn't know it then. This was the normal I knew, and it was the life I lived. I had no idea how far outside the box it was.

Aunt Edna was wonderful to me growing up. She took my sister and me to movies and restaurants (nobody went out to eat in our house), and she would often carry me around the house, teaching me to sing—songs like "Bye Bye Blackbird." She was constantly telling me how handsome and smart I was, and she made me feel like I could do anything, even when I was three and four years old.

One of my best memories and the reason that that house and the people in it were special occurred on Wednesdays. Aunt Edna worked at Eaton's, and on Wednesday she bowled in an Eaton's league. After bowling she would go to a deli in downtown Winnipeg called The Town 'N Country and pick up a 9x9-inch cherry cheesecake. She would arrive home about 8:50 PM by bus, in time for the *I Love Lucy* show, which started at 9:00 PM. She would walk in with a little white box tied with string: The Cake. We would quickly cut the cake into nine small pieces, and we'd all sit down to watch Lucy, while we ate the best cake ever made. I didn't realize the importance of this event until one night my aunt walked in with no little, string-wrapped, white box. They were out of cheesecake! You would have thought we just got news that a relative had died unexpectedly. The one thing that we had all enjoyed together was ripped away from us! I'll never forget that night; we bonded in our misery.

All these years later, when I think about why that cheesecake and *I Love Lucy* were so important to everyone, I believe it was because it was the only time we ate together. We never had meals at the same time. The kitchen was small, there was no dining room, and there were nine people with different schedules. This was really the one time we could enjoy something together.

Aunt Lily worked as an usher in a Main Street theatre, and once in a while my grandfather would take me to an afternoon movie there. My aunt would always take me around to all her colleagues and introduce me and fawn over me like I was a celebrity, even though I didn't know what a celebrity was. She'd tell them how smart I was, and I could feel her pride for me shining like the sun on my face. And although I didn't identify with the term yet, I felt loved. I remember my aunt in her red usher's uniform with a gold-trimmed stripe going down the sleeve and wrapping around the cuff. She looked official and in charge. She had a flashlight and wasn't afraid to use it to shine on someone who was acting inappropriately. I remember thinking that I had never seen this side of her. Even as a child, I sensed her to be timid and somewhat naïve. She would sometimes even ask my opinion on things and often treated me as someone older than my years. The confidence that gave me as a child was helpful as I got older.

Just before the show would start, after the lights had gone down, Aunt Lily would bring us a container of popcorn—not in a regular box though. It was the kind of box you got when you bought a number of items with drinks, so you could easily carry them all. I always found it odd that we didn't get our popcorn in a regular box. Years later I figured out that management knew how much popcorn was sold by the number of boxes used.

My relationship with Aunt Gladys was different. Aunt Gladys was mentally challenged. I would guess she had the mental capacity of an average ten-year-old, even though she was about twenty. She didn't think I was special. I was just another kid to her. She had a cupboard in the basement where she kept some items, including her toys that she still played with sometimes. Once in a while I would go downstairs with her, and she would take out some of those toys that, even though they were old, were new to me. I was not allowed to touch them, and it killed me. She would unpack the cupboard and always put the top box to the side; she didn't like that toy. I would look at the picture on that box; it's etched in my brain still today. From what I surmised from the picture as a four-year-old child, the box contained a donkey with a spring-loaded cowboy. It looked like you would press down on the cowboy, his legs would split, and when you removed your hand quickly, he would jump up and hopefully land on the donkey. This is all speculative because she would never take it out of the box, no matter how I would try to persuade her. Aunt Gladys was my balance in the house, and unknowingly she taught me that I wasn't special to everyone, and no matter how hard I tried, and with apologies to the Rolling Stones, you can't always get what you want.

My grandfather, whom we all called "Pop," was named by me after I watched *Father Knows Best* on TV. The son, Bud, called his father "Pop." I liked the way that sounded, and I liked their relationship in the show. My father was not someone who would be called Pop, and that disappointed me because I really liked the name. But Pop was a hat that wouldn't fit my dad. So my grandfather came to mind. Now *he* was a "Pop," and the name stuck so well that even thirty years after his passing, we refer to him as Pop. He, on the other hand, nicknamed me "Hoppy," after my favourite cowboy, Hopalong Cassidy.

Pop and I were fans of cowboy Westerns. If he was home on a Saturday morning, we'd be on the sofa together watching *Horse Opera*. He was a quiet man who never drove but walked a lot or took the bus. When he was out of his working clothes, he always wore a sports jacket. He was a thin, fit man, and I remember once a friend of Dad's saying to him, "Mr. Frederick, you're like a thoroughbred racehorse." That was a perfect description of him.

When I needed a haircut, Pop would be the one to take me downtown by bus on Saturday to Molars Barber School on Main Street. I remember long rows of barber chairs full of people getting haircuts and piles of hair on the floor; it was like a small Costco but selling only haircuts. When this torture was over, and if there was something good to see, we would go to a movie. We never talked much, as I remember, but he had a way about him that made me admire and respect him. The odd time he would speak of life "on the homestead," as he put it. I remember his telling me once about how, during World War I, government trucks would drive around the Manitoba countryside grabbing up young farm boys to go overseas to fight and mostly to die. He happened to be working one farm over, and as he arrived home, he realized what was happening. He hid in the ditch across the road, while two of his brothers went off to war, never to return. His life was a hard one after that, but he never complained.

I think one reason I loved my life in that house so much was the freedom I had as a child. I have vague memories of my parents while we lived there. They always seemed to be in the background. I don't think they took me anywhere much or did anything with me like reading or playing. It's like they were shadows, sort of there but not really. I know they worked long hours, but the picture in my mind of everyone at the house has my parents in faded black and white, while everyone else is in vivid, high-definition colour.

I wandered around the house and was treated like a young king. With my parents away at work a lot, I relied on the others to do things for me. If I needed a sandwich, someone would make it for me; if I couldn't reach something off a high shelf, someone was there for me. Whatever I needed, someone did for me. I was a child raised by a village, but not an organized village. No one was really in charge of me; everyone thought some other person was watching me, but in reality no one was. I did pretty much what I wanted. This was my kingdom.

I was a good kid, but I did a lot of things a child my age should never have done. I once rode a bus halfway downtown by myself when I was about five. I had ridden enough buses with Grandma to understand the concept, but I wanted to do it myself. So I got on a bus, and when I got far enough away that I could no longer recognize the bus route, I stood up on the seat, pulled the bell, got off, crossed the street, and caught the next bus back home. No one ever knew.

I had the freedom to be treated not as a child, but as someone special, someone loved, and someone who was paid attention to. None of those people on their own would have had the capacity to make me feel that well loved, but this collection of loveable misfits taught me what love really was.

I didn't realize how lucky I was until I was seven years old. That's when I moved into a brand-new house with my eleven-year-old sister and my parents—two adults I hardly knew. My sister seemed to know these people well, and they knew her. They had seen me around the other house, of course, and they knew my name.

They gave me my own bedroom—a whole room to myself with my own bed. I should have been living the life, but I wasn't. I was no longer a young king. I was dethroned, living in exile, not smart, not special, no longer handsome. I became an ordinary little seven-year-old boy overnight.

Not All Love Is Romantic

> Let us at least be grateful to people who make us happy, they are the charming gardeners who make our souls blossom
>
> – Marcel Proust

I recently learned that Finland doesn't celebrate Valentine's Day as a romantic holiday. On February 14, *Ystävänpäivä*—Friendship Day—broadens the range of love objects beyond lovers, in its celebration of non-romantic love. In fact, Friendship Day is recognized in many other countries, and June 8 has recently been recognized as National Best Friends Day in USA.

There must be a human need to honour the people we love non-romantically. Mother's Day and Father's Day have been celebrations for the influence of child–parent bonds since the Middle Ages, although Mother's Day as we now know it began in 1907. It's commemorated in more than fifty countries, but not necessarily on the second Sunday in May. And Father's Day has also become a global celebration since its founding in 1910, albeit not always on the third Sunday in June.

Then we have Aunt and Uncle Day on July 26 and Sisters and Brothers Day on May 2. And although we grandparents are usually able to cash in on the honours being handed out on Mother's Day and Father's Day, a day of our own is beginning to emerge. It began in USA in 1978 and is starting to make its way around the world.

Following are twelve stories about non-romantic love. We begin with the love of mothers.

RACHEL

Rachel prefers to remain anonymous.

My Mother and Me

I don't consider my husband, to whom I was married for almost forty years before his passing five years ago, to be my first true love, even though we knew each other from kindergarten.

When I think about it, my first true love was my mother, who passed away from leukaemia when I was seventeen. I haven't met anyone since her passing who demonstrated such pure and true love in her everyday roles as wife, mother, sister, and friend. My heart still aches for her after all these years.

DENISE OMMANNEY

Born and raised in Quebec City, Denise now resides in Winnipeg with her husband of forty years, still living the lockdown life amid dark prophecies. She's working on a wellness plan, zooming love to family and friends, waiting for the clouds to lift.

An Early Grace

He just wanted to get his life back on track—to resume his studies at Laval Law School and marry his Prairie sweetheart. She couldn't wait to restore some sense of normalcy in her world, and so as soon as he was demobilized in 1945, Evie jumped in with both feet and moved across the country, bringing her buoyant spirit, sharp-eyed sensitivity, and keen intelligence to set up house and raise a family. She was "Homemaker of the Year" material, in post-war parlance.

I've heard stories, seen photographs, read letters, even journal entries, about this happiest episode of my parents' life together. It was my good fortune to be born into these favourable circumstances.

Mummy greeted my arrival with elation. Love at first sight, she said. I say it was a love match, both ways, because I loved her back with my whole heart.

It's not what she said; it's not what she did. Those details are long gone, with only the faintest traces left. It's how she made me feel: safe and secure, loved and loveable, worthy of her radiant attention. Those memories are ingrained in my synapses, and in that sense, they will always be a physical part of me.

I couldn't get enough of her—the tender notes in her voice, her laugh, the light in her eyes, the touch of her hand. I was charmed, cheered, comforted, consoled.

It was for Mummy that I felt the earliest stirrings of longing and separation anxiety, with her that I had my first taste of intimacy and fresh intimations of self-worth. Even after all this time, I can yet summon those cloudy images and that balmy feeling that nothing was wanting in me.

A love like that—undemanding, uncomplicated, and unconditional—is bound to be short lived. You could say it comes with a built-in expiry date, sure to give way "at last and too soon" (as poet Mary Oliver wrote) to a pricklier interplay of personalities, expectations, and mutual appraisal. Once I perceived and asserted my independence, I stumbled into the usual generational kindling, sparking a fair amount of upset, harsh words, and tears between my mother and me. The babymoon was over.

My relationship with Mummy went through many phases over the course of the fifty years we knew each other. We weren't always on good terms, especially when I left the Catholic Church, but we were always connected. And despite our quarrels and disappointments with each other, that early beginning of unruffled tranquility and unalloyed sweetness makes Mummy the uncontested choice when I think about "My First True Love."

It wasn't until I was a mother myself that I learned what was important about my early childhood and what would remain important years down the line. The foundations of interior stability had been laid. I learned to trust, to get close, to invest in others. Those lessons have been, over seven decades, my most dependable protection against isolation, my way in to loving connections.

HEATHER DROZD

Heather has been married to Darrell for over thirty years, and they have two grown children. She works as a population health promoter, addressing factors in the community that affect people's health. She considers herself fortunate to have lived close to her mother all her life. She misses her late dad and is thankful for all the love both parents have given her.

Love at First Sight

My first love? I was born loving my mother, and I love her dearly to this day. I've read about how the love between a mother and child begins even before birth and is a bond like no other.

I sometimes reflect on the courage it takes to make everyday decisions as a parent. I know that balancing decisions that maintain the bond between mother and child while promoting steps toward greater independence are critical factors in promoting a child's sense of safety and security in the world. It's no easy task!

My mom tells a story about how my enduring love for dogs started when I was a toddler exploring our neighbourhood with her. She says I would run up to hug the biggest dogs in the neighbourhood at any opportunity. Although her strong instinct was to pull me back, she also wanted to avoid overreacting, so as not to create a fear of dogs. I know from when my own children were small how challenging it can be to ensure children's safety and wellbeing, while guarding against overprotectiveness.

Along with my passion for dogs, I loved school from my early years. My enthusiasm presented my mother with more challenging decisions, when I would insist that I should walk to school on my own or attend despite illness or severe winter storms.

Mom has always found ways to make my sisters and me feel special and valued. Although there was little money to spend, we always had beautiful, home-sewn clothes. I can still recall my kindergarten teacher commenting on the pretty homemade cookies and serviettes that had been sent for my snack. Birthday parties included pinwheel and finger sandwiches, along with artfully decorated cakes. Gifts were, and still are, always beautifully wrapped.

Mom's cooking and baking is much celebrated by family and friends. She has the ability to make everything taste extraordinary, in ways that I never seem to be able to replicate. I think she always knows instinctively that beauty in presentation makes food taste better too. Her holiday meals, set against beautiful table settings, have always stood out for me.

When I was about six, my sister, a friend, and I created a makeshift kite. We had used, of all things, a discarded cigarette package we'd found on the street. Mom appreciated our ingenuity and took a photo of us that we still have. After we'd gone to bed, she made us some stunning paper kites. I have a vivid memory of how excited we were in the morning when we found them hanging on the pole lamp in the living room.

Mom brought artistry, joy, love, and security into my life in many ways—as she does to this day. I have many treasured memories from my childhood, and I know there were countless other unremembered acts of love. It's common for mothers to perform innumerable unseen acts of love for their children every day. I suspect that, like me, many other people are able to appreciate that love and courage, both seen and unseen.

Thank you Mom! I love you always.

Not All Love Is Romantic

ANGELA ANDERSON

Angela is an avid reader, with a passion for experiencing other cultures through literature, travel, and people. Her enthusiasm for cultural exchange and human service led her to teach English as a second language in Japan and to a career as International Student Advisor at the University of Alberta. A chronic health issue coupled with a desire to be more present with her children then led her to become a stay-at-home mother. She lives in Edmonton with her husband, Scott; two sons, William and Aidan; and their dog, Teddy. And she has continued to experience the world through travel with her family. Angela's first "published" piece of writing was a story called "Spooky Night," written in Grade 2. Her dad's secretary typed up multiple copies, which were mailed to relatives.

Blooming Amidst the Rocks

Standing at the kitchen sink, my gaze touches upon the African Violet blooming on my windowsill. As I caress one of its velvet leaves and admire its clusters of violet flowers, I smile at the memory of a delighted ten-year-old me as my first love presents me with an African Violet he'd picked up on the way home from work to comfort his little daughter, home sick from school.

That sweet, spontaneous gesture of love left a deep impression on me and is one of the memories that comes to mind when I think of my father. It reminds me of the time in my life when he was healthy and strong, and I was a blessed little girl living a joyful life with two loving parents, two brothers I adored, and not a care in the world.

I have a collection of fond memories of my dad from that time. I can picture myself running to the door to greet him when he arrived home from work, being picked up, and running my hands along the fur collar of his winter coat. I loved working with him on projects for school science fairs and stargazing together. He taught me to find constellations like The Big Dipper, Cassiopeia, and The Seven Sisters. I still never miss a chance to gaze at the stars on a clear night, and I encourage my children to look up in wonderment, as my dad taught me to do. These memories make me smile and cry in equal measure because, at the age of forty-three, my father was diagnosed with early-onset Parkinson's Disease, and there began a gradual shift in our relationship, a redefining of who was the cared for and who was the caregiver.

I often refer to the story of my dad's illness, its related complications, and its effect on my life, as a saga. By that I usually mean, in part, that it is long and complicated. But according to oxfordreference.com, a saga is also defined as "a long story of heroic achievement"—a definition that also fits the bill perfectly. The details of Dad's saga of the past three decades could fill a book, and the key themes would be heroism, positivity in the face of extreme adversity, and an indomitable strength of spirit. His health saga includes severe muscular rigidity caused by the Parkinson's; erratic movement and psychiatric episodes brought on by the medications; a twelve-hour brain surgery; an emergency colectomy; forty radiation treatments for prostate cancer; glaucoma; and, more recently, aspiration pneumonia. Over the years, he's endured several hospitalizations and has been at death's door at least three times. It has been a painful rollercoaster ride, during which he has fought his way back up from every plummet. His resilience is an absolute marvel.

As a child and even as a teenager, when most girls are fighting with their parents, I adored my father. He was not only loving and kind, but handsome and strong, and he knew how to fix anything. He also had a brilliant mind and seemed to know the answer to any question I might pose. He was a master at all genres of trivia. He was charming and outgoing, connecting on a personal level with everyone he met, including store clerks and restaurant servers (which, as a teen, I sometimes found embarrassing). He'd always learn their names and strike up a bit of a conversation.

He retains those wonderful qualities to this day, over thirty years since the devastating diagnosis that derailed the course of his life. At seventy-five he is still handsome, having retained most of his hair, once lush and dark, now steel grey. His beautiful blue eyes still shine, despite no longer seeing as clearly. His brilliant mind still has the power to astound people with the strength of his memory and his knowledge of wide-ranging facts and trivia. Despite the communication challenges caused by his illness, his engaging personality has continued to draw people in. Because several of his caregivers have been from the Philippines, he picked up some Tagalog, adding it to the cache of basic greetings and phrases in multiple languages stored in his impressive brain. Countless times he has caught doctors and other medical personnel off guard by cracking jokes in grave situations that few people would consider amusing. I've learned from him how critical a sense of humour can be in living through difficult times. One of the few instances in which I've broken down crying in public was when the optometrist told me that my dad had glaucoma and had already lost much of his vision in one eye. That was a moment late in his health saga, and it was simply too much for me, considering all that Dad had already endured. I took a walk down the hall to catch my breath but broke into tears instead. Yet Dad, who had not been able to drive for nearly two decades, simply joked, "Well, I guess I'd better quit driving."

During my university years, we began a tradition of father–daughter lunches that we maintained for as many years as possible. I recall one of these lunches when he was already struggling immensely with the effects of his disease and the horrible side effects of the medications. I tried to keep the conversation light, not wanting to burden him with any of my problems, but he soon made it clear that he truly wanted to know how things were going and was thrilled to have me ask him for advice. I would think back on those father–daughter lunches often over the years, reminding myself that he still needed to take care of me, as much as the disease made me feel that it was me who needed to care for him.

In the wild, according to flowers.org.uk, the African Violet "is found growing in small packets of soil caught between rocks." Likewise, my dad has bloomed amidst the rocks of his illness. He was forced to give up his career in commercial real estate decades too soon, but in the spaces between the rocks of pain, suffering, and tribulation, his artistic side bloomed. He began writing poetry and painting. He became a published poet, winning poetry contests and self-publishing a book of poetry and an anthology of short essays on advice. In the moments in which his body could move relatively fluidly, caught between periods of severe rigidity, he managed to create beautiful paintings.

In the story of my life, my dad represents both my first love and my first and deepest heartbreak. He was the model to which I compared all prospective boyfriends. They needed to be kind, intelligent, strong, and funny, and to adore me and treat me well. Sweet, spontaneous gestures of love were important as well.

On the other side of love's coin exists the heartbreak caused by witnessing the devastating effects of his illness. I recall the moment I first felt my heart crack. I was a teen, hovering over my dad, who was lying rigid on the floor, unable to move. No matter what I did for him, he could not be comfortable. I kept my voice as calm as I could, so he wouldn't notice that I was crying. For a daughter to witness her beloved father suffer as my dad has suffered is simply too much for a loving heart to bear without cracking, and so I live with permanent crack in my heart. But the heartbreaking realities of supporting my dad throughout his health challenges have also fortified my inner strength and resilience and deepened the well of empathy that resides in me. Thankfully, like my dad, I am overall a positive person, and I, too, can manage to find humour in difficult times.

Caring for my first love also helped connect me to my life partner. My husband, Scott, tells me that the moment he knew he was in love with me was the first time he witnessed me caring for my dad. And in Scott I found the person who would walk beside me and carry my life's burdens for me when I needed a rest. I saw the depth of his kindness early in our relationship in the way he jumped feet first into the saga, ready to help in any way. Of course, he is also kind, intelligent, strong, and funny, and he adores me and treats me well—even offering sweet, spontaneous gestures of love now and then.

The windows of time in which Dad's vivid personality beams out from the haze of illness have become shorter and less frequent, rendering those moments all the more precious. During one visit to his nursing home—a limited outdoor visit due to the Covid-19 pandemic—my brother and I were sharing news of our kids with Dad. After a while, with great effort to speak clearly, he said, "Enough about the kids, I want to hear how you two are doing." Not that he didn't want to hear about the grandkids, of course, but it was a reminder to us that he is our dad, and he cares about us just as we care about our own children. It also demonstrated his compassion for others and his deep-seated positivity. Amazingly, he has never complained about the effects of Covid-19 on his life; during a time when many of us were complaining about boredom during the shutdowns, he was not allowed visitors for months at a time.

My first love taught me to find moments of levity even in the toughest of times, and to recognize that flowers can bloom between cracks in solid rock. He taught me that life is filled with both darkness and light and always to lean toward the light.

SONDRA MACKENZIE-PLOVIE

Sondra was born in Regina, Saskatchewan. At nine, she moved with her family to Winnipeg, Manitoba, and, at fourteen, to Sherwood Park, Alberta. Now residing in Edmonton, Alberta, with her husband and great love of more than twenty years and their two sons, she is at home wherever her family is. A professional writer and communications consultant, she spends her days storytelling, connecting organizations with their audiences, and sharing adventures big and small with her family. In her spare time, Sondra volunteers in her sons' school, seeks out opportunities to connect with others in her community, finds balance through yoga practice, and enjoys game nights and movies with family and friends.

How My Father's Love Shaped Me

Signing up for and then dropping out of karate class together, skipping school to get fries and hit the arcades, or talking about nothing and everything under the brilliant stars as we travelled across provinces on family road trips, some of my favourite memories are with my dad, my first love.

When I was very young, Dad often worked out of town, spending weekdays on the road. Fridays were magical for me because I knew he would arrive home for dinner. The excitement was palpable as I sat by the window, watching for the car to pull up. No matter how long he had been driving or how tired he was, Dad would step out of the car and gather me into a warm, full-armed hug, ready to hear all about my week.

I am still the girl who ran through the snow with bare feet to welcome Dad home from a business trip.

Years later, as I struggled through the challenges of the Grade 7, Dad was also struggling. Between jobs and facing a tough economy, he was often at home when I arrived from school. I didn't see the weight of his worries as he made time and space for me to unpack my own struggles.

I am still the girl who needed a shoulder to cry on when I couldn't find my place.

We moved provinces twice as I was growing up, both times for Dad's work. Both times, it seemed like the end of the world. As the son of an Air Force pilot, Dad knew the heartbreak of leaving behind one home to start over again in a new one. He also knew the right place to break this kind of news—in the car. As with any big talk we needed to have, Dad would invite me to go for a drive. He would let me choose the radio station, and we would head out for nowhere in particular. Years later, Dad revealed why he chose the car for these heart-to-hearts. Being in the car meant no distractions and no uncomfortable eye contact, which freed us to say what we were really thinking.

I am still the girl who knew what it meant when Dad said, "Let's go for a drive." And I am still the girl who knew, even after difficult conversations, that we'd be okay.

Family was everything to Dad. That's why he and Mum moved heaven and earth for us to visit Scotland—where he was born and where his parents, brother, and sister lived. I was christened in Scotland when I was just three months old, and we returned every few years for weddings, anniversaries, and milestone birthdays. We visited often enough for me to know my extended family, not just through pictures and stories, but through hugs and kisses and laughter around the table, as we were warmed by my grandmother's soup.

A few years ago, I journeyed back to Scotland with Mum, Dad, and my own children to celebrate my grandparents' seventieth anniversary. Soon after, I returned with my parents to bury my grandmother, and later, my grandfather. Grieving together somehow made the heavy sorrow of loss a lighter load to carry.

Not all losses that wound us are brought by death. Some losses are unexpected, leaving us dizzy with confusion and hurt. When Mum and Dad were struck by the betrayal of a loved one many years ago, I made a promise as a young girl that I would never hurt them so deeply. The wound that could have torn my family apart inflicted injury upon all of us, and we ached in our own ways. And although I can still feel the scar as if it were imprinted on my skin, I know that, by turning to each other, we grew closer in recovery and helped each other heal.

I am still the girl who strives to protect Dad's heart.

Dad identified as a feminist. Growing up in the 1980s, I wasn't the only kid with two working parents. But my parents' approach to marriage, which I now see as a real partnership, was unusual. Dad would cook most nights when he was no longer working out of town, and Mum would bake Sunday desserts. Dad would grocery shop and do the laundry, Mum did the ironing, and they shared the cleaning.

When I was a young woman, I found my own life partner, and at the age of twenty-one was ready to commit to him for life. Dad worried what being a young bride would mean for me. Would I drop out of university? Would I fade into my husband's shadow? We would talk in circles, arguing the same points and throwing up our hands in frustration.

At the time I didn't understand that Dad wasn't trying to limit me. He was fearful that I was placing limits on myself. Ultimately, he let go and trusted my decision. He was right to trust me. After all, he was the one who taught me what to seek out in a husband. And although my husband and Dad are very different men, they share the most important qualities: They are both loving, respectful, and supportive, and they both put their families above all else.

Now, after more than twenty years of marriage, the love I share with my husband has deep roots that support us through the challenges we face together. We grow together, bend with the wind together, and bask in the rays of joy that life shines upon us together. And with children of our own, we pass along the lessons of love we learned from our parents.

I am still the woman who pushed Dad to let me go. And I am still the woman who cried when she moved out to create a home of her own.

Dad was the first person I remember feeling unconditionally connected to, who made me feel accepted, listened to, valued. Through his eyes, he taught me how to see myself and to see who I could become.

VERNA KORKIE

Verna and her life mate, Bob, have three fine sons who have collectively begotten five even more wonderful offspring. In former incarnations, Verna was a registered nurse, the owner/operator of a disability case-management company, and founder of *Curves* in Canmore, Alberta. Her last hurrah as an oil painting artist and gallery owner is icing on the cake.

My First *True Love*

Riches to Rags to Riches

Father; Mother; Me; Grandpa; Pat, the Cocker Spaniel. House, car, white picket fence. The perfect life in Saskatoon, Saskatchewan. At the age of five, I had it all. That is, until the bottom fell out.

Fade to 50 shades of grey....

I'm Verna, and Fred—or Freddie—is my daddy. He lost his job about then. I don't remember much about my mother during this phase, but I know she was always there.

Sometimes Daddy would drive me over to where Hazel (his drinking buddy and God knows what else) lived—up the street in what seemed at the time to be a mansion. I had never seen such a grand house. He and Hazel would be inside, while I played in Daddy's car. Curling up on the back window ledge—the ledge where ball caps and Kleenex boxes were stored—I would feel the warmth of the sun shining through the glass.

One day I was inside the mansion with my dad and Hazel. What I didn't realize was that the pair was already stupid drunk when her husband returned home. The three of them got into it—both the booze and the fighting. That indelible image haunts me to this day, but not in a particularly bad way; it simply evokes enormous compassion and sadness for the little girl who witnessed the scene. I was detached as though watching a movie that I didn't understand. The big lout of a husband grabbed Hazel by her long hair and threw her onto the floor, all the while hollering and yelling at her and Freddie. The next thing I observed was the big lout's boots. Huge, dark, and menacing, those heavy boots laced all the way up. Mesmerized, I watched as one boot crashed down again and again and again, grinding into the side of Hazel's head, as she lay there helplessly. Screaming. Bleeding. Writhing in pain.

Fade to dark nothingness....

I was too young then to know what was actually happening, but I do remember living in the hotel above the Gem Café in Saskatoon, where my mother worked for "the Greeks," as she called them. In exchange, the three of us lived in one of the guest rooms, while my mother waitressed, eking out a meagre living. By this time, Grandpa's house, where we used to live, had been lost. Apparently to pay off my father's drinking debts.

One night Daddy didn't return to our room before my bedtime, causing me enormous fear and angst. But my mother reassured me, and I fell asleep. When I awoke in the morning, I felt incredible relief at the sight of Daddy in the bed with us. But the relief was short lived. Something awful had happened. Anxiety filled me at the sight. Daddy's eye was swollen shut and black, like a misshapen lump of coal lying where his eye should have been. A fall down some stairs was the reason given. But the savage truth was that someone had beaten the shit out of him.

Fade to black and blue....

Then Mom's brother, Uncle Jay, came to visit from Edmonton and apparently blew the whistle on this situation to their parents in Weyburn. Such a predicament was considered shameful in those days. You made your bed; you can lie in it. Keep a stiff upper lip. Lie back and think of England.

Saviours that they were, my grandparents arrived and extricated Mom and me from this untenable state of affairs. We were whisked off to Weyburn, to the farm where we lived until I was six, before moving into town. To the wrong side of the tracks, actually. But the second-storey, one-room-with-a-hot-plate that I shared with my mother was heaven. We were joined at the hip, she and I. I didn't see my daddy for quite a while.

Fade to the end of the rainbow....

My First *True Love*

When I was seven, I was over the moon with joy, truly, when my father finally showed up in Weyburn. Just as I always knew he would. He had come to me, and I had missed him so.

Next thing I knew, he and I were in his car and on our way to Kisby—a tiny neighbouring town where he was living. I was blissful, as Daddy took me into the General Store and bought me not one, but two beautiful, soft, cotton sundresses. Pink and red—my two favourite colours, then and now. Rows of smocking across the dress bodices attested to the fashion of the day. Can you even begin to imagine such ecstasy for a little girl?

Daddy took me for a ride in the country in his car. I felt so happy—loved and protected by his masculinity. Mom and I didn't have a car, but here was my wonderful daddy taking me for ride in his. I had chosen my red sundress for this day.

We stopped nearby on a dirt road, a prairie ditch between us and a wicked barbed wire fence. (I knew about barbed wire because I had lived on the farm.)

By now the cows were becoming interested in the two interlopers who had stopped to gaze, if not stare, at them. A black and white, almost singular mass undulated towards us, towards the barbed fence. I was fascinated as these bovines approached. But then something... What? They slowed down, slowed down some more, and then came to a complete stop. Reversing gears, they slowly retreated, hind ends first, in the direction from which they had come.

I was filled with disappointment to see them move away from me, reject me, and I didn't understand. My wise daddy explained that it was the bright colour of my new red sundress that had repelled them. Much like the matadors with their red capes incensing the bulls into a rage. This explanation took some of the sting out of the rejection I was feeling. How smart my wonderful daddy was.

Some long time later, I learned that my mother had received the bill for both sundresses and for the hotel room where we had stayed. Daddy had been living in his car, but for this special time with his little girl, he did what he could to show me he cared.

Fade to red and pastel pink…

The years went by, and Daddy never came back. He would send a Christmas card, and sometimes he would slide a $5 bill into it. Jean, my wonderful mother, was disdainful of this gesture. As I got older, she and I would laugh at his "generosity." In those days there was no such thing as legally enforced child or spousal support, so she did it on her own. And I guess that gave her the right to be disdainful—or any other way she wanted to feel.

When you don't have something, you miss it or want it, sometimes desperately. If you have it, you take it for granted. Even if it is taken away from you temporarily and you miss it, once you get it back, it doesn't take long before you start taking it for granted again. That seems to be human nature. So I didn't have a father, and I longed for him, and I missed him, and I wanted him in my life. My friends all had their dads living with the family so why couldn't I? My lifelong lack…

Mom was the only "grass widow" I knew of in our community. We never hear that phrase anymore, but it refers to a woman who is separated, divorced, or lives apart from her husband. She couldn't afford a divorce, so she just stayed married forever and lived in a kind of limbo. The only ground for divorce was infidelity, and she sure as hell wasn't going to provide that.

Fast forward to 1965. Having lived most of my life without a dad, my longing and anger were growing. The hate, the love. I wanted to confront him and give him supreme hell that he hadn't returned. I wanted to sit on his lap like daughters do in the movies and be loved as he stroked my long, dark-chocolate-brown hair. I wanted to scratch his eyes out with my ruby-red fingernails. If he had loved me enough, wouldn't he have tried harder? I want to hear his praises of me. Really, how difficult could it be to give up the drink?

* * *

And then I was nineteen, and it was the summer of my second year of a three-year nursing program at Regina General Hospital School of Nursing. A train journey with a fashionable berth to Richmond, BC, a suburb of Vancouver, was the highlight of my holidays. Aunt Eva pampered me in a way that made me feel like a princess. No—more like a queen. She brought me breakfast in bed on a tray every morning and adored me to bits. I lapped it up.

So Uncle Gordon and Aunt Eva offered to drive me to Chilliwack, an hour from Richmond. By then I knew that my father lived in Chilliwack. I had no idea where, but I did have a plan. I would confront him and get my answers. He owed it to me. And he would see what he has missed! I'd have my revenge!

I was all grown up by then, and very much aware that I adored and coveted fine things and always had. My mother had spoiled me—as is often the case with an only child—and she had done without. She had placed me so high on a pedestal that I could reach out and almost touch Andromeda.

In keeping with a nothing-but-the-best mentality that I had internalized, a dress and matching elbow-length cape had been commissioned and sewn for me. Peacock blue linen, both lined. Ramrod straight black seams on my new sheer nylon stockings. Cherry-red patent-leather four-inch stiletto heels. Makeup artfully applied. Hair perfect. These elements combined to complete a stunning overall illusion. I knew that I was a sensual, provocative knockout on that day. Exactly how I had planned it.

Stopping first at the Chilliwack Hotel—the town's major watering hole—I asked in the beer parlour if anyone might know of Freddie and his whereabouts. It was too easy, really. We obtained an address, and off we went.

My palms began to sweat, my breath was short, my heart galloping like a Kentucky Derby thoroughbred. This was it. The moment I had dreamed about and had been waiting for.

We pulled up to a house with a rather dilapidated garage at the rear. This is where I had been told Freddie lived. As I got out of the car, I could hardly breathe. My legs felt like noodles. I feared my whole body would collapse and dissolve, leaving only traces of peacock blue and cherry red spots melding together into a puddle of dioxazine purple where I had once stood.

I pulled myself together. Standing tall and straight, I knocked on the unpainted door. A few seconds—an eternity—passed. The door opened. Standing in front of me was a disheveled man wearing a faded-to-grey, white undershirt; suspenders; and long pants, cuffed to catch the flick of cigarette ash. Hair slicked back with a-little-dab'll-do-ya Brylcreem, several days' worth of hair growth on his aged face, there he stood. My father. My first true love. The one I have loved. Hated. Loved.

I recognized him instantly; he looked about the same as my memory of him. But I was not the same; the years had transformed me into an attractive young woman. Daddy didn't know me. How could he?

He ogled this apparition top to toe, with a leering licentious expression, giving me some kind of macabre satisfaction. "What can I do for you?" he smirked.

"Oh, this is going to be delicious." I said to myself. Feeling smug, I paused just long enough for him to drink me in. I looked at him haughtily and squarely in the eye before calmly stating, "You must be my father."

Shock. Disbelief. Silence. His face openly registered the gamut—and more. It was too much. His visage sagged. He was contrite. Tenderness began to replace his previous air. We stared at each other. He seemed ashamed of his bloodshot eyes, his liquor breath both stale and fresh, the squalour in which he lived. I felt choked with a glimmer of compassion as I observed this broken shell of a man standing inches from me—the same man who was once my beloved father. The on-again, off-again iciness in my heart had no choice but to melt.

A long-since-forgotten conversation transpired. Before I left, Daddy told me that the train from Vancouver made a whistle stop in Chilliwack, and he would like to see me again on my return trip to Saskatchewan. I agreed, and the appointed time was confirmed.

Fade to hope....

***

The time has come for me to return to Regina on the train. Again, I am nervous at the prospect of meeting my father—he may or may not be waiting for me on the train platform.

Slowly the big locomotive pulling its human cargo lumbers into Chilliwack and groans to a full stop. Cautiously I descend the train steps, the protective conductor aware that I would be here for only moments. Fellow passengers descend behind me, as others briskly move up the steps and onto the train.

I am afraid to look. Will he be there? Will he remember that I am coming on this day at this time? What if, what if, what if...

And there he is! My handsome Daddy! Dressed in a shabby but neatly pressed, dark-brown suit; clean, white shirt; and Homburg hat. He smiles shyly at me. We approach each other, and I am acutely aware that he is stone-cold sober. Breath fresh, face shaven, his dark-brown eyes clear and focused. What an incredible sacrifice he has made this day, atoning as best he can for mistakes made and opportunities lost. It is his peace offering to me (and, as it turned out), his lingering legacy, and an indelible memoir. In those few minutes, I know beyond all doubt that he does love me and always has. But for a faulty gene, circumstance, and bad choices, things could have been and would have been different. I forgive him. Unequivocally.

The train pulls away, and I watch from the window as Daddy, standing alone now on the station platform, gradually disappears at the vanishing point.

Fade to exoneration....

ELAINE ROUNDS

Elaine was born in Harvard, Illinois, and immigrated to Canada in 1970. She quickly became involved in the arts community and grew a twenty-two-year career as a professional weaver. Later, having expanded her artistic interests, she taught bookmaking, collage, and mail art to children and adults. (She has sent at least twenty thousand mail-art postings around the world.) Elaine has taught in Canada, USA, and Iceland. She has a long history of one-person and group exhibitions, and her work is in public and private collections in more than seventy countries. A mother of two, her other great loves are her triplet grandsons, Don, Nick, and Alex.

Grandma Kate

I adored my father's mother, Katherine Barbara Malinovsky, known to me and my siblings as Grandma Maynard. Although she died of breast cancer when I was just twenty-one, she had a great influence on my life. I think of her often, treasure my memories of her, and hold her in a special corner of my heart.

I grew up in the 1940s and 1950s—a generation that didn't express feelings—and I was an adult before either of my parents said "I love you." I don't remember my grandmother ever saying those words to me either, but I always knew I had her unconditional love. And I have no memories of being scolded or punished by her. Spending a Sunday, a weekend, or summer holidays at my grandparents' house was always fun; there was always a greeting of delight when we arrived.

Grandma had an orange teacup and a blue saucer, and my sister and cousins and I took turns drinking tea from it at mealtimes. I never had tea at home; we lived on a dairy farm and always drank milk at meals, so tea was a treat. Grandma used loose tea, and after the meal she would read the fortune of the person using the orange cup that day. She always said something that made us giggle or roar with laughter.

Grandma was a good cook, and I especially remember her sage dressing, gravy, watermelon pickles, pies, and cookies. When my father butchered a pig, we would deliver the head to Grandma, and several weeks later we'd pick up the headcheese she'd made. (She always teased us about leaving in the eyeballs.) We took headcheese sandwiches in our school lunches, and the other kids thought they were disgusting.

My grandparents used their den more than they used the living room. They had a daybed for napping and two oak rocking chairs. That was where they read newspapers and listened to the radio and where Grandpa smoked his pipe. My feet struck straight out when I sat in one of the chairs, and I had to work hard to make it rock. When my daughter was born, Grandpa brought me the chair. I loved knowing I had the chair Grandma had used for rocking her babies.

Many memories of Grandma involve the growing, gathering, and preparation of food. We went berry picking for wild raspberries and gooseberries. We helped in the garden, picking green beans, shelling peas, pulling and cleaning carrots. I watched and helped whenever possible when she canned fruits and vegetables and made all kinds of pickles. We loved her jams and jellies. My grandfather taught us to fish, and we learned to clean the fish he caught before Grandma fried them for our supper.

I never thought of Grandma as a pretty woman. She fitted the typical housewife image of the 1950s, with her print housedress and cover-all apron. She wore Oxford shoes with laces and 2-inch heels. I did think she looked nice when she dressed up, and I admired the wedged shoes she wore in the summer, which were the style of the day. I don't have many photos of her as a young woman, and of course those I have are black and white. Her crowning glory was her auburn hair, evidenced by the long braid she kept in an old trunk in the guest bedroom—a thick luxurious braid from the day she had her hair cut into a short bob when bobs were in fashion. She had a 19-inch waist before she was married. She wore a corset and camisole all her life, no matter how hot it was. When we visited, she would ask us to help her with the ties of the corset. I don't think she ever had a bra, and I have no memories of her wearing slacks.

Grandma was accomplished in the textile arts. She quilted, using scraps from old clothes. She crocheted doilies and the edges of pillowcases, made pulled-thread curtains for her kitchen, and handstitched drapes for her living room. Her button collection was stored in a Chinese basket with coins, beads, and a tassel on the lid. It was one of my favourite things in the house, and I played with the buttons almost every visit. My grandfather kept it until he died, two months short of one-hundred-and-one.

Grandma was funny. One Thanksgiving she imitated a turkey, and we all burst into laughter. (As she aged, the folds in the skin on her neck did resemble a turkey wattle.) We would ask her to do the imitation over and over again; it was sort of like Carol Burnett's Tarzan call, and we couldn't stop laughing.

Families were getting TV during the 1950s, and professional wrestling was popular. I loved watching wrestling with her, even though she had the sound up very loud because she was hard of hearing and didn't wear hearing aids. She was extremely vocal about the wrestlers she liked and didn't like and whether the referees were fair. Even at home, I was allowed to stay up past my regular bedtime on Thursday nights to watch wrestling, so I could talk it over with Grandma the next time I saw her.

I have the desk that my grandparents kept in their dining room—a secretary-style desk like one that a Victorian woman might have in her bedroom. The front folds down, with lots of cubby holes for paper and envelopes and a drawer for pencils and pens. The desk is refined and delicate, but when my feet didn't yet touch the floor as I sat in the chair, it seemed huge and full of treasures. I was fascinated with the quill-type pen and bottle of black ink I was allowed to use. Grandma also kept her old curling iron there. She demonstrated how she and her sisters used the curling iron, and I remember some mishaps when I ended up with singed hair. Playing cards were stored in the desk, and we all loved playing Canasta. I remember the New Year's Eve when my cousins, my sister, and I played Canasta until midnight. Grandma made popcorn and allowed us to use pots and pans for noise makers. By 12:15 AM, we were all tucked into bed.

As a young child, I was aware that my grandparents didn't share the same religious beliefs. She was Catholic, but Grandpa seemed indifferent or even scornful of formal religion, and they didn't attend church. But Grandma showed us her rosary, and she quietly bowed her head to say a silent grace before eating. Later in life—around the time she was diagnosed with cancer, I believe—my grandparents joined a Lutheran Church. The morning of her funeral, my sister and I were alone in the room with the casket. We put her rosary in her hands and never told anyone. We both knew how much Catholicism meant to her.

Grandma told me about the death of her son, Harold, and how painful it was. I was aware that her grief never really went away. I often thought that her grandchildren had brought joy back to her life after such a tragic loss. She certainly loved having girls in her life after having only boys.

Grandma was happy when I went to university, although I wasn't able to see her as often then. She was interested in anything I had to tell her. Those were the years when she was suffering from breast cancer, and she talked about it openly at a time when many people only whispered about cancer—especially breast cancer. My visits became precious, as I did not know how long she would live.

My grandfather became Grandma's devoted nurse during her illness. And when she died, he stepped up and filled the role she had played. Even when I moved far away, he always remembered birthdays,

Christmas, and other holidays, and he always wrote interesting letters. My family was blessed to have him for another twenty-five years.

Katherine Grace was the name I chose the day my first pregnancy was confirmed. I felt that the baby was a girl from the beginning, and Grace was the name of a beloved grandmother on the Rounds' side of the family. Grandma would have adored my daughter as much as she adored me. So many times in my life, I have wished that Grandma and my daughter could have known each other—especially when Katy's triplet sons were born.

The greatest gift my grandparents gave me was their time. I was truly blessed to have them. And yes, there is no doubt—Grandma was my first true love.

W. D. (BILL) VALGARDSON

Bill is a writer and retired professor who lives in Victoria, BC. He has been published in a variety of forms of literature: short stories, novels, drama, poetry, essays, and articles. Raised in the area of Manitoba known as New Iceland, he has delved into its history to create and share the world in which he grew up. His latest novel, *In Valhalla's Shadows*, is a perfect example.

Innocence

I fell in love with my grandmother just after I was born. How could I not? My mother was sixteen when she became pregnant and married, and my father, the culprit in this domestic drama, was nineteen. My mother was seventeen when I was born. She had no idea what to do with a baby—specifically, a boy baby. She'd had two brothers, but one had died from birth defects at six months and one at two years. As an only child in an English-Irish-Scots neighbourhood, my mother's experience of all other Manitoba ethnic groups was limited. She would never have met my father had the Icelandic settlement of Gimli not had daily train service, a wonderful beach, and inexpensive lots where city folks could build cottages at reasonable prices.

As with most things in life, my parents' fate developed from inconsequential details. My father's father was a carpenter who regularly built houses and cottages, and my mother's parents needed a cottage built and hired him. My father was around fifteen at the time and was working with his dad. My parents, those impulsive, romantic (and it turns out), passionate teenagers managed sex, a pregnancy, and a secret marriage. They confessed their misdoings and moved in with his grandfather, a cantankerous widower. That lasted for a winter. Then my mother's parents, even though they had little money themselves, purchased a house for them and made the mortgage payments.

I was named for one of my grandmother's dead sons. It was, I'm told, a common thing to do. Deaths before inoculation and antibiotics were frequent. Graveyards testify to the ravages of polio, measles, smallpox, whooping cough, pneumonia, tuberculosis, cuts that turned septic—a wide array of diseases that we no longer fear today. In some societies, children weren't named until after they were a year old. There was no point in naming a child with a one-in-three chance of its being dead before the year was out.

To make matters worse, my mother was very ill with eczema—so bad that she had to be soaked out of the sheets in the morning. My father, although he worked and supported us, still hadn't grown up. Drinking, fighting, and gambling were the centre of his world. My grandmother,

Irish Protestant to the core, determined not to lose another male child, took me in hand. Times were different in those days. People are shocked when they hear that in the USA, children were sent by post from place to place. It was cheaper to buy stamps and hand children to a mailman than to pay their train fares. In my case, I started travelling from Gimli to Winnipeg and back on the local bus when I could still be put in a box. My mother put the box on the bus. My grandmother met the bus at the depot. I don't remember that, but I do remember being very small and sitting on a bus seat that was way too large—too small to look out the window—and the relief I felt when I heard my grandmother's voice as the bus driver led me to the door.

My grandmother knitted and sewed clothes for me. As I grew older, she introduced me to the larger world of the city. She took me to Eaton's and bought me goldfish. On at least one occasion, she bought me a turtle. She took me to the Hudson's Bay basement, where we dined on malted milk and hot dogs. Once each visit, she took me to the Eaton's dining room, where we always had turkey and French fries with gravy. This was a treat denied to most of my school friends. Many of them right into their teens had never made the 60-mile trip to Winnipeg.

She took me to the museum, where we looked at and discussed stuffed bears and buffalo. She took me to the art gallery.

During my first years in school, from 1945 to 1947, there were no eye tests for school children. Halfway through Grade 3, we had an eye test, with the result that I was shipped by bus to Winnipeg, and my grandmother took me to an ophthalmologist. I was legally blind in my left eye, had 80 percent vision in my right eye, and my eyes didn't work together. My grandparents paid for glasses. I had gone through the first two-and-a-half years of school unable to read what was on the board, even when I was sitting at the front of the classroom. I assumed that everyone saw what I saw: an indistinct blur. I had spent those years in isolation, keeping myself amused by fantasizing. I hadn't learned to read. I couldn't see letters. The teacher said that this blur was an A, that blur was a B, etc., but I couldn't tell one blur from the other. The teachers concluded that I was stupid.

My grandmother, visiting with us after I got my glasses and realizing I couldn't read, taught me how to read using the newspaper comics. She patiently sat with me on the living room couch as I learned the alphabet and how to sound out words. When I was in my late fifties, a professor and chair of a university department was having tea with my mother and me, and my mother said, somewhat sheepishly, "You know you started talking coherently before you were one. We didn't understand that meant you were intelligent." She would have been eighteen at the time and had a grade ten education. My father had quit school before he finished grade eight.

Few people had cars, but sometimes a person with a car would be making the long trek to Winnipeg, and my mother would be able to get them to take me. That was much less frightening than the bus trips. These were the war years, and there was a major airbase two miles outside of Gimli. Young air force men were traveling back and forth on the bus in large numbers. Often they were drinking. Even though my seat had been paid for, I was often pushed out of my seat by an airman. The buses were so crowded that small canvas chairs were put in the aisle. On some occasions when I was pushed out of my seat, the driver took me up front so I could sit on the flat hump beside him. No seat belts in those days. If they'd had bus miles like we now have air miles, I'd have collected enough to have a free trip to somewhere like Regina.

A family story about one of the car trips: I'd been led to the side door of their house, my grandmother opened the door, and I said, "Here I are,

Grandma." And here I was. Safe once again. Not abandoned in a strange city with no way of finding my way either to my grandparents or back to my parents. Safe after travelling through the night into the unknown, travelling down strange streets, sometimes stopping at the houses of strangers for a quick visit but never knowing where I was. It left me with a lifetime of nightmares that are always the same: I'm lost in a strange city and can never find my way home.

Safe in a kitchen with the lights on, with the certainty that there would be green grapes and chocolate milk in the fridge. Safe, knowing that I'd go to sleep in a warm bed and wake up to a cup of tea and an egg in a cup—a soft-boiled egg stirred up with salt, butter, and small squares of white bread.

I loved my grandmother so much, this small woman with the sharp nose and the thick Irish accent, that I didn't stop holding her hand in public until I was nearly thirteen, and then only for fear of being seen by my schoolmates and teased. In spite of that rejection, she found me my first real job with United Grain Growers, and she and my grandfather provided me with a place to live every summer as I worked at the warehouse. Later, they provided me with a place to live when I went to university.

She died of a heart attack while I was on a course at the CBC in Toronto learning how to write radio drama. She had been in bed, got up and asked my mother to get her something as she had very bad gas. She sat down on the living room couch, and my mother went into the kitchen to get Epsom salts. When she returned to the living room, my grandmother was dead.

She'd travelled a long way. The daughter of a well-to-do farmer in Northern Ireland, saying yes to my grandfather's letter asking her to marry him. My grandfather had emigrated from Ireland to Winnipeg before the war, joined the militia, and was sent to France, where he was first gassed and then wounded by shrapnel. At the end of the war, he was shipped to Canada, where he spent six months with a serious infection from the shrapnel wound. He'd met my grandmother when he was on leave and visiting his family in Ireland. She said "yes." She would come to Canada and marry him (and I have a postcard of the steam ship on which she made this journey), but it would have to wait. Her mother was dying of cancer, and she was taking care of her. She said she'd come after her mother died. And she did. And she had three children, Billy, Norman, and Rae. She lost Billy and Norman, and she and my grandfather lost their house during the depression. She told me that after these three things happened, one day she was standing on a street corner in Winnipeg on a cold winter day when a fancy car went by. In it was a woman with two small children, and she said to me, "I asked God, why her and not me? Why does she have everything, and I have lost my children and my home?"

All her life, she held me tight, afraid that I would be taken away like her two sons. She loved me without reservation, and I loved her back. I knew that no matter how dark the night, nor how frightening the trip, she'd always be there at the bus stop or in a warm, well-lit kitchen that smelled of Irish scones, and I'd always be welcome.

JOANNE KLASSEN

Joanne's first love was her Uncle Willie. But she moved from her home in Ann Arbor, Michigan, to Winnipeg, Manitoba, in 1975 for another true love: Ted. She says that career, children, grandchildren, travel, and looking from her balcony at the river, no matter how wonderful, pale in contrast to the hair-raising adventure of true love.

Uncle Willie and Me

It was raining. Somebody knocked at the door, and Daddy and I went to see.

"Willie, what are you doing here? Come on in. Peg! It's Willie. How come you're not in Maryland at your Navy base?"

He walked in and stomped the rain off his feet on the mat.

"I had to get out of there, Don. I just had to. Who's this cutie?"

I looked up from where I was leaning against Daddy's leg. This man who looked like Daddy was smiling down at me. His shiny, black shoes were dripping on the rug. He had white pants and a white shirt with a little bib on the back. In one hand was a white hat, like a bowl, that he plopped on my head. In the other hand he had a dark-blue bag with handles. He set it on the floor and bent down, holding his hands out to me.

"Come here and see your Uncle Willie, the handsome brother. You must be Joanne. She's a beauty, isn't she? Takes after her mother."

I looked up at Daddy. He nodded.

"It's O.K. He won't bite."

I let Willie lift me up. He smelled nice, like skin. We smiled at each other, and then he held my head to his warm shirt with one hand, like I was his teddy bear. He kissed my hair and danced me around.

"You're a lucky man, Don."

"And you're in trouble, you son-of-a-gun."

How did guns have sons?

"Can I stay?"

"Who else do you know in Michigan? Ya, you can stay."

Not All Love Is Romantic

Mama came in from the kitchen with her apron on and Donnie in her arms. Judy stuck right next to her.

"Well, what do you know? This must be Don Junior. Judy, you're growing like a weed. Come over here and give your Uncle Willie a kiss."

Judy looked at me and stayed put. Donnie started to cry and buried his face in Mama's shoulder.

"Are you hungry, Willie?" Mama asked.

"Hungry for the sight of you all, Peg."

"You look skinny," she told him.

"I'm as fit as a fighter. They work us like dogs, I tell you. I had to get out of there."

I looked over at Mike, our dog, sleeping on the rug. *How do you get dogs to work?*

"You lonesome?" Dad asked Willie.

"Half-dead homesick." Willie said.

I looked over at Donnie holding tight to Mama, and I leaned against Willie. It was nice being carried and cuddled.

Willie and I hung onto each other that night and the next day. He told me I was his sweetheart.

At breakfast we told Mama and Dad what Willie taught me.

He said, "I just thought of a wonderful scheme." Then he nodded to me, and I finished, "You be the peaches, and I'll be the cream." They all laughed, and he lifted me from my chair to sit on his lap.

I cried when Willie left. He took his white hat and put it on his head and picked up his blue bag. Then he kissed my cheek, hugged Mama and Daddy, and closed the door behind him.

Daddy reached down for me and turned to Mama. She said something about Joey's first love.

Dad said, "I think they needed each other. That lonesome little brother of mine is in a heap of trouble, leaving the Navy base like that, but he said it was worth it."

It sure was.

Sixty years later when Willie died, we were still sweethearts. Daddy's little brother lived out loud. My first love, Uncle Willie. I can still feel those strong arms holding me today.

AINSLEY A. THORARINSON S. BLOOMER

Ainsley lives in Winnipeg, Manitoba. She is married with two adult sons. She is of Icelandic heritage, and she started taking Icelandic language classes in adulthood, first at the Scandinavian Cultural Centre and later at University of Manitoba. She ended up teaching Old Norse Mythology and elementary Icelandic language, culture, and folklore—privately and in various educational venues. She is now retired, yet her passion for things Icelandic and writing led her to write a book, a retelling of an Old Norse mythological tale: *A Viking Legend: The Descendants of Odin*.

Thank You, Great-Uncle Carl Hansson

I have early memories of a loving family. At the time of these memories, I had a mother, father, and brother. And there were many elders, all of whom spoke the Icelandic language.

Great-Uncle Carl Hansson lived with us for a while, and he spoke Icelandic as well. Although our mother didn't speak the language, our father did. We used to hear Icelandic spoken in the background all the time, like a mysterious musical melody all its own, a background music I rarely attended to but knew it was there. We realized if we heard our names that our elders were talking about us and didn't want us to know what they were saying. The mysterious secret language. Unknown to my brother and me then, the musical background offered us reassurance, peace, and security. We were told that it was the old language, that we were to speak English because we lived in Canada and that English is the language spoken here. And so we were not taught Icelandic as children, and our elders even discouraged us from learning it. I never questioned anything at the time; I just went along with what they said.

I must have been about three or four, if memory serves me correctly, when Great-Uncle Carl brought out a chess board and placed it in front of me. I had no idea what it was or what he was about to do. He slowly and methodically taught me the names of the pieces of the chess board in English, explaining their special places and their moves. The castle could go backwards, forwards, and sideways in a straight line, and move as many squares as I liked. The knight moved in an L shape, in any direction. The bishop could move only on an angle, forwards or backwards, as many moves as I liked. The king could move one space at a time in any direction. The queen was the most versatile, as she could move in any direction for more than one space. The pawns could move forward two squares on their first move and one move thereafter. I thought there were too many pieces. How on earth could I remember them all and their moves? But he didn't give up on me and slowly went through the moves of each piece.

It took me a while to learn and remember all of this, but Great-Uncle Carl was patient and kind. Finally, when he figured that I had mastered his teachings, we began to play chess. We shared many games, some of which I'm sure he let me win.

My First *True Love*

As life went on, my brother and I were blessed with a sister—for my parents a beloved daughter, and for Great-Uncle Carl a beautiful niece, whom he patiently taught the skills of the chess board.

Uncle Carl also sang us an Icelandic lullaby called "Bí, bí og blaka":

> Bí, bí og blaka álftirnar kvaka.
> Ég læt sem ég sofi en samt mun ég vaka.
> Bíum, bíum, bamba, börnin litlu ramba
> fram á fjallakamba að leita sér lamba.

We never knew what the words meant, but the song and the tune have stayed with us since early childhood, and every time I hear them, I think of Great-Uncle Carl. It was not until adulthood that I sought out the meaning of the words and began to question some of our early upbringing. Why did our elders insist we learn English but not Icelandic? But that is another story.

The translation for the song goes something like this, although I am sure there are other variations of the translation:

> Bird and butterfly, the swans sing.
> I pretend to sleep, but I'm still awake.
> Baa, baa, be calm, the little children
> Wander the mountains looking for lambs.

I didn't realize it then, and maybe Great-Uncle Carl didn't realize it either, but he instilled a love of learning in me and a love that was patient and kind. It wasn't until adulthood that this realization came to me, and I am forever grateful for his love and teachings, which have stayed with me to this day.

As an adult, I have had the opportunity to pass on some of his teachings. I taught chess to some friends and to my children, and I have taught a bit of elementary Icelandic.

I understand that there are different types of love, and there are different types of first true love. This first love that Great-Uncle Carl freely shared has endured. For many years, these special memories were lost within me, as the pains of life took me in other directions, yet the memories were eventually revitalized and blossomed and have sustained me. Hopefully I have passed on a little of his love to you, the reader.

Great-Uncle Carl has long passed, and I wonder now if I ever thanked him or told him how much I loved him. I would like to take this opportunity to tell him now, wherever he is.

I love you, Great-Uncle Carl, and I thank you for your loving kindness and your teachings. And I thank you for "Bí, bí og blaka."

SODHI PILLAY

Sodhi's early childhood began in the small rural town of Tugela, Kwa-zulu Natal, South Africa. After graduating with an MCom, she spent fourteen years working in corporate finance before journeying to Edmonton, Alberta, to take up the rewarding fulltime position of wife to her supportive and loving husband, Vincent Pillay and full-time mother to her wonderful sons Dhiren, Santhan, and Khirthin. When she is not pursuing her passion for cooking, entertaining, reading, or writing, she can be found on interesting catchup conversations with her mother (Dhana) or Benny's Bunch (her siblings' group on the messaging app, WhatsApp) or ardently trying to win a game of Scrabble with her soulmate, who still gives her butterflies in her tummy and bunches of star gazers from grocery market flower aisles. Sodhi's story is about love of a family—a family headed by the inexorable Dhana.

Benny's Bunch

I always wondered whether procrastination or patience shrouded my birth into my mother's world. A world and everyday reality that was fraught with hardship yet grounded in immense love.

My mother vividly recalls that when it was time to deliver me into this world (as if I were a posted parcel from another life, except with no "return to sender if undelivered"), she carefully fed my six older siblings, took crisp, dried clothes off the wash line (no washing machine would feature in our household for another thirteen years), and summoned the midwife to let her know it was "time."

Home deliveries of the birthing kind are sought after nowadays; for my mother, however, it was a necessity borne of the fact that money was in short supply, and having six other healthy children meant that her birth canal was a busy highway for most of her childbearing years. Hospitals would have been the tollgate serving only to hamper an otherwise placentally smooth process.

In the warm comfort of a winter's afternoon, I made my debut, screaming into the world, aided by the strong contractions of my stoic mother's resolve and the midwife's steady, capable hands. The deliverer of all parcels, big, small, boy, girl, good disposition, or bad disposition, the postmaster of our household, my Amazon mother, was integral to the survival and thriving of our family tribe.

I was born in a time when home delivery meant a home birth and not an Amazon package appearing at your doorstep. Takeout meant a leftover, home-cooked meal from a neighbour's pot, when neighbours knew your blood type and family tree, and fences did not prevent the flow of life and information. A time when your neighbour's children were like your own, and discipline, nutrition, hand-me-downs, and praise could be distributed without restrictions. Community did not mean the area code you came from, but rather a place where you belonged. *Ubuntu* (a Zulu word that refers to community spirit—"I am because you are") took root like the baobab tree, rooting birth, death, success, and failure within our rural South African community.

Our home was a simple construction of cement floors, wooden planks nailed together, and a sloping tin roof. The wooden planks, like unfaithful guards, would allow the elements to infiltrate on windy, rainy, or hot nights. The furniture was basic and functional. If it was not something that could be sat on, slept on, worked on, or packed with, it was not needed or could not fit. If we had been aiming for a minimalist décor, we achieved it without even knowing.

Our house stood like a dwarf beside the great umdoni tree. The tree stood solemn, stately, and green. In the spring, it would unleash first yellow buds, and, as the days grew longer, it transformed into bunches of green berries, a useful tool in the ammunition cache for our rambunctious childhood games. At the peak of the summer, the green berries would ripen into fleshy purple fruit that yielded a sweet flavour and a stain that would remain on our clothes long after summer was over.

This tree would stand unyielding to the rain, wind, sun, flood, and drought. It would exhibit our amateur graffiti art etched on its bark and hold our weight as we climbed or swung from its strong branches. It was a tree of my childhood that came to symbolize the cycle of life and death.

My father's emotional pain was rooted in the loss of his own mother at a tender age and the untimely tragic death of his sixth child, aged five. My sister, whose life, though brief, touched everyone's life in a profound way, would unravel his carefully curated emotional faculties. His brilliant yet fragile mind could not bear the weight of his own sadness. Sadness and grief that were unfathomable and growing like a cancer would eventually lay claim to his soul and blot out the love and dedication that was alive and affirming all around him. The intense love that my mother and all his children shored up for him could not penetrate his fortress of emotional pain. Our family grew increasingly weary, exhausted from watching my father's tumultuous battle with inner demons, and we were all hopelessly ill equipped to help him. Only at university, some eight years later, would I stumble onto a subject called Psychology, and then I would understand that my father's malaise actually had a clinical name: depression.

The umdoni tree seemed to step in benevolently to shield our family from our father's self-destructive path. The tree that gave us an abundance of its life season after season would one day offer up its very branch to our father's tortured soul so that he could end his pain.

The tree would come to serve as a reminder of what we lost, until eventually we packed our good memories, sadness, anger, and love and turned our backs to escape its menacing testimony of choices made and childhoods ended. I was ten years old, but I felt like my emotions had aged me beyond my chronological age.

As a child growing up within the close proximity of love's dichotomous effects of destruction and dedication, one would think I could lay claim to emotional scarring. Thankfully the wonderfully sheltering kindness of a tight-knit community and the fiercely protective attitude of my mother and siblings ensured that my love story drew its strength from all that was demonstrably good and solid in the world.

We did not utter the word "love" frivolously while growing up. It was an intense, personal emotion that seemed to give gravitas to a mysterious force that guided my mother's every decision, every selfless or creative act to clothe us, feed us, and keep us safe. This caring, nurturing, protective instinct oozed from every pore of my mother. We did not need to hear the word "love" to know at a cellular level that we were loved. The rich abundance of my family's love deftly loosened the noose of poverty that often threatened to choke the dreams and aspirations that floated in my young head.

All my good memories would feature a strong, steadfast, hardworking, disciplined, kind, loving mother and siblings, who seemed to have an ecosystem of love and nurturing that sprouted and thrived organically around me, drawing strength and inspiration symbiotically as we progressed from childhood to adulthood. Experiencing poverty, success, death, and life side by side, my nuclear family gave me the freedom, space, platform, and strength to become a force of love in my own world.

It is within my family unit that I experienced what it meant to love and to be truly loved. My first love will always be my amazing, sometimes dysfunctional, but love-worthy family. My early experience of unconditional nurturing and love fashioned my ideas of romantic love and later my own mothering love for my wonderfully special three sons.

I remember the many times I had to wave goodbye to my family, and how the longing to be in their happy, accepting, nurturing, funny, kind, strong presence would gnaw at my insides. The sadness too great for my heart would contort itself into a lump that would be lodged at the bottom of my throat, making it impossible to escape the visceral taste of sadness. I was conflicted with the desire to see and experience the great big world, while wanting never to leave the reach of their physical closeness. Euphoric at my personal growth, while longing for the confines of my love bonds, I would oscillate like a pendulum between these extremes during many personal and career-developmental milestones in my life that placed physical distance between my family and me.

Love forms the foundation of relationships and connections that resiliently thrives, no matter how great the distance or the time apart. Wherever I journeyed, their love followed like a faithful guide, propping me up when my resolve faltered and when fear threatened to topple me.

From my first love, I learned that love does not mean constant agreement, but the validation of being heard, understood, and acknowledged. I learned the power of sharing my space, my resources, and my time. I learned how to be a cheerleader, mentor, and peer. I learned how to love with an unconditional heart and how to heal a broken heart.

I learned how to allow my heart to grow to include new additions to our ever-expanding family. Most importantly, I learnt from my first love that when I met my soulmate across the Scrabble board, that (apart from the butterflies creating havoc in my tummy and all high-scoring words exiting my brain), I would feel a sense of belonging and unconditional acceptance. My heart would have found the coordinates to my starboard—a home to lay my passions and dreams and a home to let my guard down.

Our capacity to express love, the form it would take, the intensity, authenticity, and truth of a full expression of all of who we are, springs forth from a love reservoir that we begin filling when we enter this world. This entry can sometimes scream procrastination or patience. I was lucky enough to win the lottery of birth and to be born into Benny's Bunch, where a broken or a healthy mind was rewarded with a lifetime of unconditional love that lives on in our hearts long after our bodies or minds succumb to the vagaries of life—and sometimes the vagaries of love.

Not All Love Is Romantic

SHIRLEY YOUNKIN

Shirley has lived all her life in Ohio, except for her first few years of elementary school, where she had the good fortune to encounter Miss White, who was later chosen Alabama Teacher of the Year. As a math teacher and vice-president of a small business, Shirley has spent her adult life surrounded by numbers; yet she has learned the power of the written word (and a spouse) to enlighten, inspire, and enrich. Shirley has also written about her husband Dave, in the section entitled "Love That Lasted."

The Wonderful Power of the Written Word

Birmingham, Alabama, 1954. I was a small-town Ohio second grader who had been transplanted to the Deep South for three years and was about to leave my beloved teacher, the caring and genteel Miss White, to go back up North. To make the transition a little easier, Miss White gave me a Fuzzy-Wuzzy book entitled *Snowball*. It's about a little white poodle named Snowball, who, through a series of misadventures involving rabbit holes, coal bins, road tar, and much more, becomes increasingly black, hence fuzzy. Well-meaning but less-than-helpful acquaintances make suggestions to Snowball's owner to remedy the situation, including potent baths, mountains of "maple leaves, picked in Spring" and "oatmeal, cook it slow—that will make the color go," but to no avail. In the end, the owner finally decides to accept the inevitable because "It's not everyone who has a black Snowball."

The book itself was a thoughtful gift, but the letter written inside was priceless and poetic, describing how Miss White would "miss your beautiful black curls, bobbing in laughter" and "your reading because you read with such thoughtful, intelligent expression." I never gave up SNOWBALL, reading to my own children the very tattered and not-so-fuzzy book (with my own second-grade letter to self to "have a happy happy day").

The book is gone now—though available on e-Bay—but the memories of that loving teacher and her inspiration to love books will never fade.

TANYA SPEIGHT

Tanya was born and raised in Kingston, Ontario. Her passions include animals, reading, writing, and music. She spent twenty years in Toronto, where she worked in the music industry, then in politics, and then as Communications Coordinator at University of Toronto Students' Union. She now lives in Perth, Ontario, with her sister and brother-in-law and her two beloved cats.

Love in the Therapy Room

It astounds me that there is only one word in the English language for "love." As a lifelong English student and lover of languages, I have contemplated this issue endlessly. With myriad ways to express "angry"— enraged, mad, seething, seeing red, irate, cross, incensed, furious, bitter—it's a wonder we haven't evolved to the point of expressing love in the multiple ways it hits us.

There are infinite ways to love. We love our parents, our friends, our homes, our pets. We love trips we take or a great plate of spaghetti. And perhaps one of our strongest forms of love is for these screaming, pooping, vomiting little chaos makers, our children.

The first time I felt love was for my parents. And likely, at the same time, my older sister. We're hardwired to need love from our caregivers for our very survival. It's funny that this most primal form of love isn't what we first think of as "love," when in actual fact romantic love comes much later.

I loved my first dog. Lake was my best friend, my big, furry comrade. We played hide and seek, chase the tire swing, and catch the stick. In the evening, when I was tired, I'd bury my face in his belly and snuggle in on the living room carpet while my parents talked or tidied in the background. Lake was my second love.

The night he died, we went to pick out a cat. It was an easy choice—she was the only female in the litter, and we wanted to have kittens. I couldn't wait! We brought Melody home and kept her in one room—my sister's room—to ease her transition. I sat on the floor for hours, quiet as a mouse, trying to show her that I was safe, we were safe, that she could come out from under the bed. Watching this tiny creature trembling and terrified changed me somehow. My heart poured out empathy. I fell in love in a new way that night. Different from my love for the goofy and fearless black lab who'd been there since before I was born. This was pure protective love, like she was my new baby sister, and I promised to keep her safe forever.

Melody did eventually come out, and so began a thirteen-year relationship that I still treasure more than thirty years later. Melody and I were inseparable. She followed me from room to room. I dressed her in dolls' clothes and pushed her around the house in a baby stroller. And when she finally did have kittens, she chose to have them in my bed in the night.

"Mummy! Daddy! Melody brought a mouse into my bed!" My dad sat up and looked at my terrified face. "Wait a minute…," he said, and we all tiptoed back into my room to watch the babies being born. Of course I learned a new kind of love for the tiny babies I'd seen birthed.

And on it went, with every little nonhuman creature I've shared my life with, a new kind of love for each one.

The same pattern emerged as I progressed through best friends in school, got to know aunts and uncles and cousins, found and lost lovers, and travelled to different places. Always new ways to fall in love.

But what happens when you fall in love with your therapist? It's such a cliché that we brush it off as not real or use clinical words like "transference." But love in the therapy room is very real; it's one of the most real things I've felt in a long time.

I've had my fair share of trauma. I've been abused—sexually, emotionally, physically. I've lived through panic, anxiety, depression, and dissociation. I've had therapist after therapist; some have helped me, and some have harmed me. I've opened up just a little bit more in each therapy room, only I didn't know what I was opening up to until recently.

My current therapist is a long-time expert on abuse and trauma and their lingering effects, and an extraordinary human being. I can count on my weekly sessions with her to be gentle, caring, and completely safe. I have never known such safety before. How could I not love it there, and love *in* there?

In her article, "Falling in Love in Therapy," Christine Hutchison describes the therapy room as "an incubator for love"—a safe place to practise "the feeling and the skills of loving." It's a room in which any emotion is allowed, "including love and hate, rage and gratitude."

Not All Love Is Romantic

The very fact that loving a therapist is a cliché means that it's common—and real. There are online communities and chat rooms for people who have fallen in love with their therapists. Their stories are similar. Their therapist has proven to be a supportive, kind, nurturing presence in their lives, and they long for that understanding outside of the therapy room. Their therapist has all these special qualities they've never found in anyone else. And they long to reciprocate, to be able to care for their therapist, to know how their therapist's day went and offer words of advice.

People have asked me if I'm in love with my therapist. I guess I talk about her a lot. And I've given it a lot of thought, I really have. *Am* I in love with my therapist? Yes. In the same way I'm in love with a beautiful tree that touches the sky, or a view of the lake with no land before the horizon. She's purely and simply a God-given miracle—whatever you perceive God to mean—something precious I can't help but love.

But what is it about her that I love? I don't actually know her outside of the therapy room. Can this be real love? Well, I love her compassion for people, her ability and *willingness* to understand any situation, her empathy, her outlook on life, the twinkle in her eye, and her sense of humour—and most of all her gentle and reassuring way. She allows me to open my heart, feel some love, and be myself in the process. She has a vibrant, positive, and relaxed energy that feels good to be around. I love her perspective when we talk about world events. I love her charm, her wit, her ease. I love everything I know about her.

But what kind of love is that, really? Can it really be romantic love, given that I don't really know *her*. What I do know is what I see in the context of her helping me. No, this is yet a new kind of love. After months of analyzing our relationship and my feelings for her, I had to admit to myself that one significant thing I love about her is the way she sees me.

She listens to me with keen interest. She never judges or argues. She encourages me to be honest, no matter what comes out. She gets my humour. She sees my strength. She shows compassion when I cry. Her opinions of and reactions to me show me that I'm funny, brave, and smart, and that I can make my life a joyful experience. How could I not love a person who gives me all of that?

So am I in love with my therapist? Yes, in yet a new way to love someone. Our entire relationship is about me, my needs, my story, my healing. But feeling such a rush of love in the presence of my true self shows me the possibility of actually loving myself. My therapist has opened that door for me, and it's up to me to walk through.

The hours I've spent in the therapy room with her have taught me how to breathe, how to accept what I'm feeling, how to allow my feelings to flow through me without resistance or judgement. For dealing with panic, my therapist has taught me how to identify the fear underneath. For dissociation, she has taught me to slow down and feel each movement in my body, bringing me back to myself. She has taught me how to relax, how to ride the waves of anxiety, how to process my past. But most of all, she has shown me, by example, that I am loveable.

Therapy has shown me a possible world in which I *don't* need someone else in order to feel loved. I am seeing all my own loveable qualities bounced right back at me. I'm opening up to myself. That's what the therapy room is all about—learning to love yourself. And now, instead of worrying about a future without her help, as I have for so long, I find myself fantasizing about a future in which I don't *need* her help. Because my future some day will not include her, and as much as I'll miss her, I can't wait to fall in love with myself.

For the Love of Cuddling

> Nobody has ever measured, even poets, how much a heart can hold.
>
> – Zelda Fitzgerald

The depth of emotion and the detailed descriptions of storytellers who told about their non-romantic love experiences are testament to the fact that not all first true love is romantic. It now becomes clear that not all first loves are even human. If there is a theme here, that theme is cuddling or—as revealed in our first story—not cuddling.

My First *True Love*

JAMIE KOSHYK

Jamie lives in Winnipeg as part of a large, loving clan. From an early age, she has been drawn to young children, and she relishes her roles of mother and grandmother. Over the past forty years, she has taught and researched in the field of early learning and childcare. Jamie has always dreamt of moving to her grandparents' farm in Libau, Manitoba, and living with many, many dogs. Her current puppy love is the cuddly, calm "Winnie."

My Lovely, Snappy, Snarly Snoopy

"Get in your box!" she would yell, usually several times in a row, while pointing to the side door that led to the back entrance of our house. Snoopy would slink down the few stairs but with a defiant air. I would follow behind my mum, and when Snoopy went into his box in the alcove where we kept our shoes, I would sit on the stairs beside him. The door to the main part of the house would close, and then, through tears, I would tell Snoopy, "She doesn't mean it." I would try to soothe his feelings, but after he had growled and snapped at my hand the first time, I had quickly learned not to try to pat him. So I sat near him while he glared at me, daring me to try to comfort him.

I loved, loved, loved my first dog. I remember watching my dad running in the rain from the car into the house. When he took his coat off, there in the palm of his hand was a tiny Chihuahua puppy. White, with black ears and a black spot on his back. He WAS Snoopy! He was so small that he had a hard time walking on our linoleum floor in the kitchen. My younger siblings and I sat on the floor excited, laughing, and totally enamored with the new addition to our family.

Who knew back then that Snoopy would grow into an unaffectionate, temperamental dog? He was small and tough. I think in another life he was a big, mad dog. Snoopy had a ferocious bark and would chase cars down the street, trying to bite at the tires. He destroyed many shoes, including Auntie Louise's when she came for a visit. I don't ever remember cuddling with him. He wasn't sentimental. But we all enjoyed watching him race around the living room when my dad came home and would clap his hands, saying, "Peel, Snoopy, peel!" One of our favourite family stories, in fact, is how fast Snoopy would run around the entire room; it seemed that he was running on the walls!

The summer I turned twelve, we moved. Snoopy didn't come with us. I remember asking many times why he couldn't come and not letting any reason sink in. The day soon came to say goodbye, and I shed many tears. My heart was broken. I still have Snoopy's collar and license stored with other treasures from my childhood. For the past forty years, my siblings have teased me about those mementoes. But my love for my first dog was strong. Even if he was a growling, snappy, un-cuddly dog, he made his way into my heart.

TIFFANY BERMAN

Tiffany loves exploring life and the world with her family. A lifelong traveller, born in Ann Arbor, Michigan, and raised in Winnipeg, Manitoba, for the past twenty-eight years her home base has been outside Washington, DC, where she has worked, studied, married, and raised a son and daughter. After a career in environmental science and law, Tiffany now focuses her energy on creative projects and reconnecting with her beloved pastimes of softball, gardening, travel planning, and genealogical research.

Pure Comfort

As a child back in the 1970s, I wondered who my first love would be and what would my first love be like. What would my first love like about me? How old would I be? What would it be like? I was more of a tomboy than a girly girl in those days—but even tomboys could not escape the pop culture that was and is full of images and ideas about such things to fill youngsters' imaginations. Although it wasn't a preoccupation for me, I distinctly recall reflecting on these questions from time to time in my younger years.

Fast forward to 2024. I am beginning the second half-century of life. It feels like it has contained several lifetimes of highs and lows, a winding path that's not always been easy but has almost always been good. I wonder whether most people my age would agree, as I do, with Eva Cassidy's lyrics: "I never thought it would turn out this way."

I've had some serious relationships, but I waited until my mid-thirties, after graduate school and a successful career in Washington, DC, to settle into family life. I've been married for twenty years to a fantastic, hardworking, fun and funny guy I met doing one of my favourite things: playing softball. We were pitchers on opposing teams who met in a collision on the third-base line. He tagged me out when I tried to steal home from second base on a long fly ball. (He loves to tell people that his team won by one run that day.) We have two kids, a nice house, and a comfy lifestyle.

I didn't experience love at first sight on the third-base line that day or in earlier years of boyfriends or with any other person. Like many things in life, my first love didn't fit a movie storyline, magazine cover, or classic tale. To my great good fortune, I didn't have to wait until adolescence or beyond to find it. I didn't have the anticipation of waiting for someone to call back, the agony of disappointment, or the struggle of finding a way forward after a first fight. My first love was pure, unconditional comfort in the form of a small black cat.

In the middle of my kindergarten year, my parents divorced, and my mother moved my younger sister and me with her to central Canada, a world away from our family and circle of familiarity in the USA. For my sister and me, it was like moving to another planet. We felt incidental, isolated, limited, alone. I asked for very little, except for a pet—something and someone of my own. I'd never had a pet, and the building where we lived in Winnipeg didn't allow pets. But as soon as we moved from our small apartment to a house, I told my mother, "It's time for my cat"—words I love to this day.

The little two-year-old cat was the most beautiful creature I'd ever seen, with her silky, short fur; shiny whiskers; and light-green eyes. We met her in a park, where an older lady, her first owner, explained that she could no longer easily care for a pet. We probably weren't the best cat caretakers at first. It was a learning process for all involved, and perhaps for the cat it was what for humans is sometimes called "character building." Whisky learned to let me hold her and hug her, and she comforted me during the many times I needed her. She unfailingly came to me when I called her, played with me, slept on my lap, and was a perfect companion. Given the number of my troubles she soaked away over the years, it's amazing that she lived for almost fifteen years. Without her, it somehow feels like I might not have survived that long.

There's something deeply and incomparably comforting about a relationship that doesn't involve words, conversation, negotiation, compromise, organization, planning, or thought. There are no politics, budgeting, scheduling, or disagreements. It is almost meditative, existing only in the space of the right now. It is the experiential embodiment of Thich Nhat Hanh's words, "Our true home is in the present moment. To live in the present moment is a miracle." Simple comfort in the form of unconditional, unromantic companionship can melt away time, space, and the outside world.

I'm not sure if I agree with the Bible verse that says "Love never fails." More my style is "Love never dies." Love changes, and relationships can come and go. But our experience of true love, and especially first love, stays with us. We are drawn to revisit it in memory and try to recreate it the present day. I have a great husband, but I also have a small, silky, black rabbit that is my comfort and delight. True love and true comfort live on.

VIVIAN ANDERSON

Vivian is a proud mother of three (four if you include her fur-baby) and grandma of five. She enjoys cheering on her grandchildren's sports teams, attending their music recitals, and generally celebrating all their milestones and accomplishments. She has been singing in her church choir for some twenty years, a talent that surprised her, having believed all her life that she could not sing. Other hobbies include reading, gardening, and attending live theatre.

Love at First Sight

My precious little Honey had passed away in March, and I was determined not to get another dog until the fall in order to save money, as

I had many vet bills for Honey in her last couple of years. Still, every once in a while I would look on the Internet for dogs available in the Edmonton area. I wasn't going to get a puppy this time.

One day in early May, I saw the picture of this little non-shedding one-year-old dog (a poodle–shih-tzu cross) on Zoe's Animal Rescue site. Her little face captured me right then and there, and I was determined to get her. I was meeting friends for dinner and had to call to say I'd be late so I could complete the extensive application form and submit it; it was long and detailed to ensure that applicants knew what they would be getting into by adopting a dog. I received a call soon after submitting the application to advise me that I was one of three applicants selected for a home visit.

A few days later Lucy (then Ruby) arrived for her home visit. My sister-in-law, Nina, was visiting me at the time. When the worker and Lucy arrived, the dog came running in and jumped up on the couch and made herself right at home. The worker advised me that one family had withdrawn their application, so there were now just two of us. Lucy and the worker stayed for quite a while, and Lucy went out and explored the back yard and met the neighbours. She seemed right at home. They finally had to leave to go to the other home and meet those applicants.

The volunteer who was boarding Lucy called later to say Lucy was mine if I still wanted her, and of course I was thrilled. Apparently Lucy didn't even want to go into the second home.

She was delivered to me at the end of the May long weekend. The volunteer who had been caring for her was in tears because she had fallen for her too.

I changed her name to Lucy because we already had a Ruby dog in our family, and she was mine from the minute we got home. She is an amazing, loving dog. Even my vet says people wait their whole lives for a dog like Lucy.

She loves kids and any adult who will give her some pats or cuddles, but she is mine first and foremost, following me everywhere when we are out. She watches when I am getting ready to go out and is sad when she can't come with me. She sleeps with me, and in the morning gets under the blankets with me for our morning cuddle. I make sure, when we are on our walks, that she is right at my side when we cross streets, so if one of us gets hit by a car, we both do.

I feel very blessed to have this little dog to share my days.

* * *

NOTE FROM NINA: I had never realized that dogs could fly until I saw Lucy shooting through the air toward Vivian. Clearly a match made in heaven.

MAUREEN MORRISH

Maureen served for over four decades as a front-line worker and counsellor for Youth at Risk. After retiring, she moved to her cottage in a small lakeside community, where she lives with many birds and wildlife; her cats, Olive and Girl Stan Lee; and her dog, Sarah Jeannie. She enjoys fishing, bird watching, and dabbling in writing, and she is self-employed as a Tarot Card reader.

The Gift of Heartbreak

This story is about love. A love so deep that when I lost that love, even the Universe knew that it was time for an intervention.

My mother worked late, my three brothers were all older than I was, and I was a ten-year-old latch-key kid. So when I arrived home after school, I would unlock the door to our suite, let myself in, and hang up my key necklace. And my best friend Trib was always waiting for me. Greeting me with a big yawn and long stretch, presumably just waking up after her long afternoon cat nap.

We were inseparable. Trib had filled the position of parent, sibling, and best friend; she would sprawl out on my homework on the small kitchen table and even had her own cereal bowl set beside mine. Before heading off to work, my mother would place both our bowls on the table, along with that morning's cereal. After school, weather permitting, I would take Trib down to the riverbank behind our apartment, and we would roam and play amongst the trees and labyrinths of thick trails. We had become as one.

One day she went missing. I called and searched for her for almost two days. The pain was so intense that even during my sleeping hours, I was searching and calling for her. On the second morning, I was awakened by her meowing to be let in, and I bolted out of bed, opened the apartment door, and ran out into the hall and down the long corridor to the back outside door, truly believing my beloved Trib would be there. That long walk back to our suite was heavy with disappointment. I was consumed with heartbreak so devastating that I vowed never to love again.

A friend knew of my agony and asked me to go to church with her the third day of Trib's disappearance. Our family never went to church, but we did pray. My mother had taught us about the power of prayer, so I figured a church would add more power to my prayers.

I don't remember the description of the church, but what I do remember is seeing the most beautiful woman I had ever encountered as a ten-year-old. And still now, in my sixties, I've never experienced anything as beautiful. I was standing, singing a hymn. You know that feeling you get when you know someone is looking at you? If you don't, it is a sense, a feeling, an energy shift. Well I had that feeling. I turned to look, and there she was. Glowing, illuminating, not a glow so super bright that I needed to shade my eyes, but a warm, loving glow. She had an aura around her that kept in that white energy, encased her as if to keep all the earthly sins from her pure love and long hair and small, kind smile. She was like a living porcelain statue, without the heaviness of such weight. The angel was sitting there for me to see, hands folded in her lap, and she began to tell me telepathically, "Do not worry about your Trib; she will not be coming home. She is safe and will be fine. I am here to tell you that."

For whatever reason, I turned away from her and stared straight ahead. Not sure if it was fear, shock, or pure amazement that made me turn away. When I slowly turned my head back to the angel, she was gone.

I left the church and ran all the way home, running the scenario through my mind. I burst in the door and blurted out to my mother what had just happened. She carried on folding the weekend laundry, listened intently without doubt, and when I was done telling my story, she hugged me, held me tight, and allowed me to cry in big air-gasping sobs. My mother reiterated what the angel had said about my cat not coming home. And added that it was probably Trib who asked the angel to pay me a visit. I have since had a dozen or more cats as friends and companions, but I have never loved one quite like my Trib.

CAROL (REEVES) PAUPTIT

After a ten-year career with a Toronto investment firm, Carol has spent more than a quarter century volunteering with a caring-and-sharing organization. Travel was a big part of her life until the late 1990s, when she and her husband Carl build a summer home in Prince Edward Island. When Carl retired in 2010, they began spending their summers on the island. The pace is much slower there, leaving her time to enjoy golfing, cycling the Confederation trail, bird watching, walking the beach, and enjoying the therapeutic water. Spending time with friends and family (especially her three granddaughters) is an important part of her life.

A Treasured Possession

As I sit and ponder my first love, thoughts of my childhood come to mind. I'm the youngest of six children, born on a farm on Prince Edward Island, on November 3, 1945.

My most vivid memories are of sharing chores—weeding the garden, picking strawberries and raspberries, tramping down hay in the loft, and picking potatoes. During potato harvesting season, the schools were closed for three weeks so the children could help. Money was scarce, but Dad paid us $4.00 a day. We were very excited at the end of the season to order our winter clothes from the Eaton's catalogue. No thought of toys!

Christmas was a time of family celebration, with an abundance of food. We were accustomed to receiving one small gift from Santa and a stocking filled with ribbon candy, nuts, oranges, and apples. (Fruit was a treat.)

When I was eleven, I wondered if Santa would come that year. None of my siblings were hanging their stockings. They had the usual goodies on a dinner plate.

On Christmas morning, I couldn't believe what I was seeing! A beautiful, 24-inch doll wearing a pink dress, a pink bonnet, and white shoes. Her short hair was auburn, and very curly. She was my very own—not a hand-me-down from one of my sisters. I named her Tracey. I knew that very day I would love her forever.

I left the farm when I was nineteen, and Tracey came with me. She was loved by my children, and I saved some of my daughter's clothes for her. She visited one of my granddaughters for about six months. But now she is back with me, wearing one of my daughter's dresses. My memories give me great joy as I look at her in the pink Queen Anne chair in my bedroom.

FRED ANDERSON

Fred's first career was as a manager and executive in Canada's real estate industry. He then formed his own property development company. For his third career, he drew upon his strong literary and artistic skills, resulting in two books: *White Flashes on Charcoal* features his poetry and artwork; *Keep it Cold* is a collection of sage, inspiring, and witty pieces of advice he and other contributors have received over time. Fred has three children and five grandchildren. He lives in Edmonton, Alberta.

Loving to Death

Roisogle. That was my father's name for this bird of the marshlands, more generally known as a bittern. It was anything but beautiful, coloured functionally bland to blend with the brown and green of cattails and other marsh vegetation. It had a call like the sound of a sump pump and a face that only a mother could love.

It happened like this: My father and I were out muskrat trapping in Netley-Libau Marsh. As we turned over our canoe to start off in the water, a little baby bird was staring up at us from the jungle of shotgun shells, wax paper, brown paper bags, and the crusts of yesterday's lunch. We'd obviously interrupted his meal. I immediately felt an attraction mingled with pity for this bird. At our trap in the next muskrat house, we saw remains in the form of bones and feathers of an adult bittern—obviously the mother of this little bird.

I was five or six years old then, when I took this Roisogle into my care. With it, I was experiencing the first stirrings of love for a pet. We had outdoor farm dogs, but they served the function of herding cows and were never considered pets.

I found a spot for my Roisogle in the chicken house, by then devoid of chickens and used as a storage shed. The next item on the agenda was food and drink. I went on the hunt. That year the leaves on our farmyard were being devoured by armyworms. I supplemented the worms with any bugs and grasshoppers I could find. I even tried him on bits of sweets: raspberries and cranberries that I found in the bush. Finally, some water in an old pot completed his meal. I felt a great sense of responsibility for the bird, especially for keeping it out of the hot summer sun, and

I scurried all over the yard to find sustenance for it—my beautiful pet Roisogle, on this hot mid-summer day, with high humidity.

I was exhausted and nearly sun-stroked from all my outdoor labours. I had to go into the house mid-afternoon to escape from the heat, but I made sure to let my mother know that she should check on the bird if I fell asleep. When I awoke at 4:00 or 5:00 PM, my mother was sitting beside me on the bed, her hand gently on my shoulder, saying, "Fred, I have some bad news."

The lurch to my heart was strong and deep. I had big plans for the two of us, but I must have overfed him. He died from too much love and care.

From that experience with my first love for another being beyond my family, I was left with a life-long caution to temper my adoration. And I have never again loved anyone to death.

ZEN SIGMUNDSON

Zen was eleven years old when he wrote this story. He and his parents and younger brother live in Winnipeg, Manitoba, and have a cottage in Lake Forest, near Gimli, Manitoba. Two outstanding things about Zen are his deep love of animals and his involvement in the martial art of Aikido.

Struby: The Cat in the Basement

My first love was my cat, Struby. I got her when I was about six years old. My dad's friend had a cat, and his daughter was allergic to cats, so they had to give Struby away. She was very old when she came to live with us, and she died about two years after we got her.

Struby was light grey with dark grey spots—lines of dark grey—very fluffy. She had green eyes. And she had a grey spot on her forehead.

Struby lived mostly in the basement. I think she was kind of scared of our dog. So every day I'd go down to see her and sit with her for about thirty minutes to an hour. I'd just pet her and bring her food and water, and sometimes I'd give her treats. She always made me happy. When I was in a bad mood, I'd always go down to the basement to see her, and she'd make me feel happy again.

I kind of thought of Struby as my cat. Other people in the family would go down to see her, but I was the one who went down to see her every day. I thought of her as my best friend.

GUY ANDERSON

Guy has worked in IT for the Government of Canada since 1997, a career choice that brought him and his family to Ottawa twenty years ago. His interests involve hunting, fishing, and training his dogs. He returns annually to the family marsh-side cottage in Libau, Manitoba, to recharge his batteries. Although he is well past eleven now, that's how old he was when he wrote this story.

My Hamster

One of my best friends in the whole world is Sandy. Sandy is sort of a peachy-beige-coloured hamster. Below is a drawing of what he looks like:

My First *True Love*

Sandy's name isn't really Sandy; it is short for Sandstone Peachfuzz Colwill Anderson. I bought him in September 1981, just after school started. I still remember the day I bought him....

I had been begging for a hamster for years. Now all the crying and sulking had paid off. I didn't want to get a hamster at Woolco because the night before I had seen the cutest little hamster at Eaton Place, but Mum said, "I'm not willing to drive all the way downtown if I can drive a few blocks to Woolco."

When we arrived at the pet store in Woolco, I went straight to the hamster section. I saw a cage full of hamster babies and picked one I wanted. Then Mum said I couldn't have a baby hamster because I'd be taking it away from its mother too soon. I went over to the next cage where the hamsters were a little older. All the hamsters were huddled in a corner. I picked one. The storekeeper reached in the cage, but the one I picked ran away from him. All of a sudden the runt of the litter (Sandy) ran up to the storekeeper's hand and sniffed it. I said "No. I've changed my mind. I want that one." So the 'keeper put him in a box, and we drove home.

After I had Sandy for a while, he became so good that he would obey my every command. One day I came up with a great idea—to give Sandy an allowance. I figured that he should receive one-eighth of my present allowance of $2.50. That means he would receive roughly 32 cents each week. As Sandy started to behave better and I received more allowance, he was up to 50 cents a week. I decided that with the allowance that I had saved up, I would buy a present for Sandy, and with the allowance Sandy had saved up, he would buy a present for me. Now Sandy is a regular member of the family. On certain days he will buy a present for certain people. For instance, on Mother's Day, he bought Mum an Agatha Christie book.

I could go on and on about my hamster, but I will just say he is the best darn hamster-person in the world.

Love Knows No Bounds

> Of course it is happening inside your head, Harry, but why on earth should that mean that it is not real?
>
> – J. K. Rowling

Not all first loves are romantic. Not all first loves are cuddly. Not all first loves are living things. Following is a wide array of stories from eighteen people whose first love was bestowed on neither a person nor an animal.

The first two stories in this section were especially intriguing to me. I was surprised to learn that two women—a city girl from England and a country girl from a farm on Prince Edward Island—shared the same true love: their white figure skates. But when I mentioned this coincidence to my friend, Marion, she expressed no surprise. She said, in fact, that that was probably her first love as well.

My First *True Love*

BLANCHE CLOW

Blanche was known for decades as a hard-working Prince Edward Island farmer, but she's currently enjoying her retirement. Although she's heavily involved in her community and her church, her family is and always has been her priority. She loves socializing (to which I and anyone who knows her can easily attest) and taking tours and bus trips with friends. A healthy lifestyle is important to her, and she always manages to find time to keep active.

My Skates: Loved, Loved, Loved My Skates

I grew up on a farm with five brothers. Needless to say, my first love was certainly not going to be a boy!

There was always a huge amount of work to be done on the farm in the 1950s and 1960s—just as there is today—and we were all expected to do our share. In the fall, it was potato-picking time, and students on Prince Edward Island had a two-week break from school to help with the harvest. (I often wondered what students who didn't live on a farm did during that time.)

Potatoes had to be picked at home before we could go out and earn money working at other farms. Earning $4.00 a day was like gold to us at that time.

Winter clothing was supposed to be the priority for our hard-earned dollars, but one year it didn't happen that way. I needed new skates desperately, and I took some of my money to buy the most beautiful pair of white skates ever seen! I had learned to skate on my mother's skates, and they weren't white; they looked like BOYS' skates. My new skates came from Smallman's Department Store. They cost $13.95. Now, I was reminded that this money was not wisely spent when winter clothing was needed so badly. But cold or not that winter, I dearly loved those skates and kept them polished shiny white.

On Saturday afternoons I would walk into Summerside to the rink with my brothers, Woody and Carl. We would skate for two hours and walk back home—an 8-mile round trip.

But it was worth it.

I'm sure I had the best skates on the ice.

I would often find ice patches in the field or at school—another chance to skate!

As time wore on, those skates did wear out, but still I loved skating. My husband gave me skates for Christmas one year. I graduated to adult skates and still enjoyed that feeling—skating to the music, sailing across the ice.

After breaking my leg and spraining my ankle twice (not by skating), I realized that it probably wouldn't be a wise move to try skating again. But it's tempting to relive my first love: Those Beautiful White Skates.

CHRISTINE SMITH

Christine is a retired financial advisor, now free spirit. She lives in Canada but discovered her first true love as a child in Bournemouth, England. Although she grew up in an entirely different world than Blanche Clow did, Christine shared the same first love.

Jumping, Spinning, Gliding

So often sleep eludes me. Nothing helps! I've tried drinking warm milk and honey, rubbing my feet with magnesium oil, fumbling my way down the hall to my darkened bedroom, counting sheep...nothing works... nothing helps. One night, as I lay there, trying not to look at the clock, my thoughts took me to the ice. Back to my youth, floating across the rink, jumping, spinning, gliding, completely lost in the music. A peaceful joy came over me, thinking back to the days when nothing else mattered in the world. I could remember my whole program and skated it flawlessly.

It wasn't an easy transition. It certainly wasn't love at first skate.

My friends and I had decided to try our luck at the local ice rink. After I had rented a battered pair of black skates with ratty laces and blades that hadn't seen a sharpener for weeks, perhaps months, we hobbled onto the ice, clutching the boards. Our feet had minds of their own as they slid in different directions. We watched as others gracefully passed us, as we fearfully held onto the boards, not daring to let go. After getting nowhere fast, I decided it was time to be brave. I gingerly took one hand off the boards and took a couple of steps. Steps, not slides! My ankles bent as I nervously removed my other hand and attempted to glide. Crash! I was soon sitting on my bottom, feeling very numb. After dragging myself up, I started again. Down I went again. Stubborn to the core, I kept on. One slide, both feet out from under me, down on my bottom, again and again.

Finally, after what seemed like hours, I discovered the knack and started to make progress. Bit by bit, step by step, I started to skate! I was hooked.

The next Saturday, my friends had moved on to easier challenges, but I was back at the rink. It didn't take many Saturdays before I was a skater.

I knew the key was a decent pair of skates. After much pleading with my mother, I raced to the rink the next Saturday clutching enough money to buy some skates of my own. I can still see myself that day, proudly walking to the pro shop and asking to try on a pair. They were gleaming white with shiny blades. Sitting there lacing them up was one of the happiest moments of my life. After the blades were sharpened, donning my smart blade guards to protect the edges, I walked to the ice. I first noticed that my ankles weren't bent in half anymore, I felt supported. I thought the whole world must be admiring me and my smart skates.

I stepped onto the ice. Crash! I was down! What happened? This wasn't the way I was supposed to make my entrance. I didn't know it then, but I later realized that I had skated only on blunt blades. My new blades were so sharp they took my feet right out from under me. Undeterred, I carried on and soon adjusted.

Every week was the same. I couldn't wait for Saturday. I leapt out of bed, gulped down my breakfast, and raced to the rink. I was one of the first on the ice. I didn't stop for lunch; nothing could induce me to leave the ice until the final buzzer sounded.

As time went by, I convinced my mother to buy me a membership to the rink, explaining that it would be cheaper in the long run. I booked lessons every week with Jack Santell and started taking all the tests and entering every competition. Nothing else mattered in life. I had found the perfect love.

Over the years, nothing has come close to that feeling of bliss. Skating was my first true love and still holds a special place in my heart. In the darkness of my bedroom, I still feel the elation. It's just as strong in my heart as ever. I am back with my first and only true love.

My First True Love

KAREN MINDEN

Karen is madly in love with her grandchildren, children, husband, extended family, and life in general. She has enjoyed several varied careers, first as a scholar of Chinese politics and Asia Pacific economic relations; later as the founder of Pine River Institute, a mental health and addiction treatment centre for adolescents; and most recently as advisor to several youth treatment programs. In 2010, she received the Order of Canada for a lifetime of service to our country.

Clear, Crisp Love

I was born after World War II in a peaceful country to a loving family. I was surrounded by adoring parents, grandparents, aunts, and uncles. And apparently I was a very affectionate and sociable child.

I can't remember a particular first love except for one food—celery. Celery was easy to eat, crisp, clean, subtle, never cloying, and not too filling. I had a rather sensitive stomach and a small appetite, and I didn't like strong flavours. I recall that my favourite part of eating hotdogs was the bun, and I would dispose of the wiener. But celery was always easy and pleasurable to eat. I didn't have to hide my uneaten portions under the table or slip them to the dog.

Thankfully, I eventually evolved into a normal eater, after some years of struggling with too little or too much food. But I always have a supply of celery in my fridge. And I prefer a higher ratio of celery to eggs or tuna in sandwich fillings.

ULLA ERIKSSON-ZETTERQUIST

Ulla is a professor of management studies, University of Gothenburg. Her research interests centre on organizing, especially technology, governance in professional organizations, diversity, and inclusion, in a variety of organizations in the private and public sectors. She has published journal articles, research monographs, and textbooks in the field of organization theory and management studies.

Truly, Truly Loving Reading

Reading books has been a central activity in my life since I was very young. I remember sitting in front of the television, which was located in a bookshelf, deciding to read all the books I saw just as soon as I learned how to read. This love for books was a passion I shared primarily with my father and my grandparents. My mother was the one who read out loud to us, but given that she was an entrepreneur, along with running the household, she had less time to read for her own pleasure.

When I was ten years old, I was completely enthralled by Enid Blyton and read every story I could find about the adventures of the Famous Five. The dangerous mist hastily sweeping in over England's fields is one of many images I will carry with me for life, along with an image of the fat, yellow, apparently delicious milk the Fives were provided with at their numerous farm visits.

My female classmates were all six months older than I was and had the kind of maturity that came from having older sisters and brothers or just from having parents younger than mine were. A big theme among them when we were ten years old turned out to be "love," defined as who these girls would be in love with. The subjects of their devotion often changed overnight. As we lived in a small society, the number of boys considered eligible for this love was also limited.

I was completely disinterested in these ongoing discussions about love and managed to ignore them for a while. My disinterest included my classmates' affections of the day and their discussions about what would be the best gifts for these the young men—gifts such as candy, 10 cents a week, or other minor things. The boys never asked for these gifts (maybe because the young boys were as immature as I was); they may have served as a token of the girls' own feelings.

Then came the day and the moment when the girls would no longer allow me to escape. "Ulla, tell us who you are in love with." I had no clue, whatsoever.

"Ulla, come on, you have to tell us. Would it be XX, or YY, or...?" No, definitely not.

And finally, the ultimatum: "Ulla, you have to tell us by tomorrow, or else...."

There it was! I had to come up with something. The solution turned out to be rather easy. Of course it had to be the dark, clever, caring, wise, responsible, and kind Julian of the Famous Fives. Dick could have been an alternative among the five, but he had been introduced as being less handsome and less clever, and although very witty, he was not an option for this situation.

My answer the next day did not impress them. During the upcoming days, I had to describe Julian in detail and explain why I was in love with him. Then they decided that Julian could not be a proper subject for my affection, and I was once again given the ultimatum. This time I came up with a name of a boy one year younger than we were, somewhat shy, who would not be involved in the social games of the kids. This boy was never my love of any kind, and absolutely not a love similar to the one I dreamed of having with Julian, but he did serve well as a disguise. The girls stopped bothering me about love, at least until he and his family moved away.

One part of my first true love still remains today. It is not a character in a book, but rather the pleasure of reading books. And for many decades, I was lucky enough to be sharing numerous readings with my father.

STEFAN ARORA-JONSSON

Stefan Arora-Jonsson describes himself as a middle-aged Swedish man. Currently holding the Chair of Organization and Society at Uppsala University, he previously worked in the field of development aid and as the technical attaché of science and technology at the Swedish Embassy in India. He is the surprised husband of Seema and the proud father of Sebastian and Maya.

A Summer Romance

One summer, when I was six years old, I got a beginners' fishing rod. It was mint green with a silvery reel. With the rod came a lure shaped like a fish, with a tri-hook trailing behind. It was made in a translucent plastic with silver glitter inside. It was beautiful.

Like all the summers of childhood, this one was permanently sunny and lovely. But weather didn't really matter to me, in any case, as I had my rod and my lure. I fished. And I fished. And then I caught my first pike. In the larger scheme of things, it was not a big one—barely big enough for eating. But I had caught it. And to my young eyes, it was enormous. This fish proved that the lure and I were meant to be.

Summer progressed, and as all fishers know, lures get caught in things other than fish. I climbed trees, waded through slimy undergrowth, dipped my head, and felt tentatively along rocks with hands and feet. I didn't know how to swim, but I did what I needed to do to keep my lure from danger. It was mine. It was precious.

My best friend and fishing companion was my younger brother, Örjan. He was four or five at the time, so he wasn't always allowed to go fishing with me. But when he was, we were always together. One day I allowed him to try casting with my lure. To make sure that it wouldn't get snagged and lost, we went far out on a dock. (Far, in our minds. It was probably about ten metres.) And, like any excited child, he forgot caution and snagged the lure. Into my bare shin. I remember my beautiful lure swinging from my shin, stuck deep with two hooks. I cried. My brother was scared and ran to get my father, who took me to the local hospital emergency room. The doctor told my father that he was going to press the hook so that it broke the surface of my skin and then bite off the barbs with pliers—that this was the easiest way of getting it out. I cried. Not out of fear, but at the thought that my lure would be ruined. I forbade them to wreck it. And my stubbornness saved my precious lure. They gave me a local anesthetic and made a small incision in my shin that allowed them to remove the hook unharmed. (I now realize that a new hook would have been simple to replace. My six-year-old self did not see that reality; he saw only the destruction of his beloved lure.)

I lost the lure not long after. It was no one's fault. The line snapped when I was casting, and the lure sank without any possibility of retrieval. I had lost my first true love.

I didn't think of this as a "love" at the time. But close to a half-century later and after thirty years with my second true love, Seema, I see the signs. Like any true love, this lure made me a bigger person, a braver person than I might otherwise have been. It also taught me that love can be lost for no reason, without being anyone's fault. It can just happen. And as with any other loss, I had to learn to live with it. It was hard when I was about to turn seven.

I'm over it now.

DEBORAH SCHNITZER

Deborah is a retired smoker and professor of English, engaged in community learning and human rights education as co-founder of the Living Story Project, Writing as a Tool for Transformation, and the Canadian Institute for the Study of Antisemitism. She's a writer, film maker, co-editor on collections of life writing, and Baba with a wild and warm heart to the magnificent Sybil Inez and Lev Mendel. As Deborah tells me, "Writing this story reminds me of the path taken after my first love and I broke up more than thirty years ago. I survived, grateful that the affair met its dissolution."

cigarettes

At ten. Rothmans.

I write this as the adult Deborah who knows more, who understands that cigarettes are bad for you. I am seventy-three years old, and I have not smoked cigarettes for twenty-nine years. Ex-smokers carefully track time. They know exactly when they found that first cigarette. How long the initial love affair lasted. When they had to give it up.

At ten, in a crazy family most interested in throwing things at one another and screaming, cigarettes had my back. They were in the trenches with me as antidotes to pain. When I was quite little, my mother blew smoke in my mouth as a way to sedate toothaches. It worked. The home remedy transitioned: I added inhaling to ease other aches and pains. First, I stole a Du Maurier from my mother's red and gold package in the black plastic purse with the silver clasp. She did not notice. Not that she ever said. Then I stole two.

From the first puff, euphoria. I did not sputter. I did not turn green. I did not throw the cigarette into the toilet bowl in disgust. Rather, I took a second puff. A third. The girl who was "just looking for a fight," who had raced into the bathroom with that sour puss—the one who was "gonna get it if she didn't smarten up"—calmed down, puckered, inhaled, and smiled. Neither crookedly nor stupidly. No. She put her elbows on the counter in front of the mirror; her face rearranged itself more completely. She dreamed a little, discovered a best friend, discovered she was not alone.

At first, I could afford to sneak only one or two cigarettes. From my mother and then from an older brother or his friends, when they left their packages where I could see them in their black and gold leather football jackets or on the back seats of the cars they were taking out for a spin on a Friday night. Although they were casually invested in their smokes, I already understood that smokes were something magical. In a world turning upside down, a world of bullying and broken glass, cigarettes softened sticks and stones, melted mean words.

A single inhalation, maybe two, and whatever else was being pushed down my throat—so that I would do as I was told or shut my mouth—dissipated. One small, slender stick filled with tobacco, gently rolled between thumb and index finger, a coal burning brightly at its end, warm wind floating inside my chest, smoke curls through the bathroom window, the door locked, another slender stick, one more.

What could cigarettes do? I figured almost anything. Put me to sleep, untwist springs, settle disputes that had daunted me in day's light. Flip of my lighter in my own bedroom. Inhale. Wait for that bit of a burn at the back of my throat, flick with my tongue a stubborn tobacco flake stuck to my lip, smoke-thickened, honeyed breathing. A slower rhythm. Exhale. Quietude. Out and about, cigarettes raised my voice expertly in conversations that might have been beyond my reach had I not been fortified, elevated. Smoke in my eyes, a puff above like a crown, queenly with new friends playing hooky.

What would I not do for love.

To support us, I became very good at locating loose change, nickel and diming my way into a 40-cent single pack, Rothmans, rather trim in blue and white, cellophane unwrapped, hidden in the back of a second drawer, wrapped in tissue. Each cigarette better than the one before; each moment alone—bathrooms, behind garages, sequestered in secret places on the way home from school whose alleys I would never disclose—release. If I smelled different, no one said. There were so many casual smokers, so many others with lovers of their own, I seemed to blend in. Even at ten, eleven, twelve. Certainly at fourteen. A cigarette in hand, at the corner of Pim and Queen Streets, past midnight, beyond curfew, a match struck, the flame wavering in the wind, rolling paper catching fire, the first draw. Unbeatable. Billboards behind me, illuminated by passing headlights, dancing down to the last drag.

My first true love saw me through tantrums and disordered eating, marriage, pregnancies, and graduate school. Our luck lasted. If my breathing became spotty, my voice pebbled, if my children joined Quit Now campaigns in their classrooms, if I was fenced off in public places, if the cost skyrocketed, still I could proclaim my love. That's what friends who become lovers do. They stick together. Even if it hurts.

And then there is this day. It can come at any time. When the best friend, the lover, tried and true, shows its truer colours. Shows one's own. The habitual is understood as the habit that can kill. The camouflage sags. The mirror cracks. Every cliché comes to the rescue, and the little girl of ten racing into the bathroom for cover is seen anew by the adult Deborah who knows more, who figures it's time to treat that little girl a little bit better.

The day may begin at the dentist's office. A root canal, the intention to quit never clearly articulated. The root canal demands that smoking cease during the day. Withdrawal. Unbearable. But the desire to cheat is thwarted by the vigilance of children at the diner chosen to celebrate the end of the dental appointment and the six hours without a smoke that follow. *Can I sneak one?* The children's faces are full of faith. The waitress serves with kindliness, seeing my fidgeting, the gum wrappers, a mother sweating, the purse too close in her lap. "Bidis." That's what she'd found at O Calcutta, an import store on Portage. "Cut the edge. Transitioned right through the worst of it." She writes it down. The name.

It's Friday night, and O Calcutta is still open. I race inside and purchase a little packet, cone-shaped, prettily wrapped. Tiny triangles inside. Eight. I've lit one and inhaled it before I'm back in the car. Euphoria. Immediate. A piece of cake, this quitting. I open my eyes. My children are beautiful. My car is beautiful. My husband is completely perfect.

What are Rothmans by comparison?

If it weren't the children's bedtime, I would insist we return to the diner and shower the waitress with kisses. Triple her tip. Ask her if she would like to live with us. Pay her tuition. Upstairs, after "night night," another little triangle, more sublimity. There is nothing I cannot do… until the seventh little triangle is ash and I discover at noon the very next day that there are NO MORE BIDIS at O Calcutta. How is that possible? What kind of conspiracy has driven the antidote off the shelves? Where is that damn waitress who set me up? What kind of monster would leave me hanging high and…

High indeed. That's the ticket. Bidis. Some exquisite form of ? and I the beneficiary. Betraying my first love for a more potent escape artist. Do I scour the city to see if there are other Bidis out there that can aid me in my transitioning? Am I to go cold turkey into an even colder night? Have I fallen off the wagon, exchanged a first love for an even more mysterious second cousin?

Dawn. I take hold of my old and new lover and the industry that made us both—the nicotine, the additives, the commercials, the ?—all the broken glass and the sticks and stones. I give them up.

It's hard to do. There are tears. Night sweats. Cravings. Binges. Not many moments go by without thinking of them, that rush, the escape into comfort, softened nerve endings. I dream of my first love hiding in the bottom drawer of my office desk, of clandestine meetings in the backseat of a lover's lane, of the smoke-screened battles of wits with my best friend in cafés, fueled further with black coffee and cinnamon buns half eaten.

Awake, I pass old haunts, head down, terrified I'll turn the handle, rejoin the crew beckoning from bar stools, waving their particular smoky lovers, signaling a pleasure not meant to last—for me. At thirty-nine, I take to another love, bubble gum, and another, my purple bicycle, and gripping the handlebars, I pedal furiously for three spring and summer months, a woman dispossessed, weaving in and out of traffic, dispensing her habit, holding on for dear life.

VALERIE PARKER MACKENZIE

Valerie has enjoyed varied work experience as an administrative assistant in the areas of education, medicine, real estate, law, cable tv, and university archives. Moves took her from Winnipeg to Moose Jaw; back to Winnipeg; to Nassau, Bahamas; Vancouver; Gimli; and finally back to Winnipeg. Today the loves of her life are her six great-grandchildren.

Comfort, Trust, Security

There is no one left to ask. A search through old photographs reveals nothing. When the love affair began and when it truly ended, I can only guess at this point. I do know that it brought me immeasurable comfort. My parents' attempts to smother and poison the relationship met with no success. The ridicule or criticism of others had no impact. When life brought feelings of rejection, fear, unhappiness, my love brought instant comfort, trust, and security. It was always with me. I gaze upon it these many, many years later and easily recall that feeling of gentle ease it provided. What else could a left thumb be for?

Love Knows No Bounds

RANDELL PARKER

Rand grew up in a military family and continued that tradition. He was an officer in Princess Patricia's Canadian Light Infantry, serving in Germany, Cyprus, and the FLQ crisis in Quebec. Rand and I had something in common: our mutual hatred for an apostrophe where no apostrophe belongs. Our plan was to travel from town to town in retirement, equipped with cans of paint for deleting apostrophes from signs that read such things as "Plant's for sale" and "Get your hot dog's here." Sadly, Rand did not live to engage in that project or to see this story in print.

The Power and the Heat of First Love

Young as I was, I had no way of preparing for the power—and the *heat*—of the feeling. Until that moment, the only similarity I had known was when Mummy tucked me into bed at night.

But when I first laid eyes on...HER...well, I was delightfully stultified, actually *warm* all over!

I had heard her name—her delicious, exciting, triple-barreled name—on the radio quite often. Something about her "figure skating" (whatever that was) was on the news every hour. But to actually *see* HER, in this full-colour picture right here in front of me, I honestly forgot to breathe for a moment. Her blonde hair, her blue eyes, and the red velvet and white fur of her outfit—unbelievable! All I could think of was to hold her and hold her and hold her.

It's the late fall of 1949. I'm five years old, sitting on the living room floor of the big old farmhouse in Falmouth, Nova Scotia, staring with incredulity at my very first, but oh-so-real love, *Barbara Ann Scott*.

Well OK, it's only a picture of a Barbara Ann Scott doll in the coloured section of the Eaton's catalogue, but still....

CHRISTINA GARSTEN

Christina is a social anthropologist with an interest in globalization and the way lives are intertwined with local and translocal influences—in organizations and in informal social circles. She is currently a professor at Uppsala University and Principal of the Swedish Collegium for Advanced Study.

Stepping into the World

When I was a young child, my family moved from a small inland town in Sweden to the big cosmopolitan city of London, England. This was a formative change for my little sisters and me. Memories from this period are plentiful and colourful. I remember sitting by a window in our apartment in the Docklands area, looking with amazement at the congested morning traffic, half hidden in heavy fog. I recall my first day at the East End primary school—the friendly schoolmates and the firm, yet welcoming teacher, Mrs. Wright, and how I learnt my first English words out of sheer necessity. Perhaps most of all, I remember the gift my parents gave me on my seventh birthday soon after our arrival: a book entitled *Min första resa runt jorden* (*My First Journey Around the World*). This educational journey in text and pictures gave me a window to the world. It fed my fantasy and imagination and broadened the context of my cultural encounters in the London East End neighbourhood school, with a new language, new habits, and other perspectives. It opened my eyes to the world and invited me to engage with it, in all its beauty and complexity.

This, I believe, is where my love story with anthropology began. And it's a never-ending story.

MICHELLE KUBE

Michelle grew up in Northern Manitoba and moved to Winnipeg when she was thirteen. She loved growing up in a small town but definitely sees herself as city person now. She tells me that she has too many interests to list, but that they would include sports, reading, writing, and an undying love for music. Music is her trusted friend, and many of her memories are based on the year a song was released. Music, she explains, allows her to feel right to the core—much like writing does.

The Music Took My Hand: A Love Story

October 1987

It won't stop.
Your leg bounces.
Up. Down. Up. Down.
You can't stop it.
The kick drum thumps in your chest.
Boom. Boom.
The rhythm forces your heart to beat in time.
Thump. Thump.

The crowd is in a frenzy. Your personal space gone, the mob screaming and bouncing. Their energy fills your every pore. The scent of stale beer, cheap perfume, and BO permeates your nostrils. The aroma laces fingers with the haze of weed as it drifts over everything—or at least that's what you've been told.

The guy behind you spills most of his beer down your back. The air is thick with heat, but you still shiver as it drips straight down, drenching the back of your underwear. He apologizes with a laugh. Your fourteen-year-old self is pretty sure he isn't very sincere.

Your beer-soaked shirt sticks to your back, and your damp bra clings to your front. Thank god you pulled your hair into a ponytail, and it's not stuck to your neck.

Boom

You're blown back when the next song starts, and the pyro goes off. You knew that it was coming and still nearly jump out of your skin. The heat blasts your face. You check your hair—it's not smoldering. Good.

Your BFF bumps hips with you, and you both sway in time. Your heads knock together as you sing the chorus at the top of your lungs.

The stage lights swirl. Your brain tries to keep up with the movement. Light beams cut through pyro smoke as it hangs with the hot body stench.

A pulse races down your spine when fingers scrape over the guitar strings. Like nails down a chalkboard but with a delicious tingle. And then the brightest spotlight ever finds your eyes, the temporary blindness annoying. When your eyes come back on, there are white dots everywhere. But that doesn't alter your need to keep bouncing in time with the beat.

And then it happens.

This is the one. The song you've waited for all night. Your rib cage struggles to keep everything contained. Your legs launch you up and down, the heavy drum forces your fists to bang to every beat above your head. Your fingers morph into the standard rock and roll horns. Your mouth goes on autopilot as the words come screaming out. You can't sing worth shit, but that doesn't matter. No one can hear you over the absolute insanity that fills the arena.

The music takes over.

Completely.

* * *

My first real concert: Michelle

The second the lights went down, the music took my hand, letting me leave everything else behind. It stole my heart from the very first count in.

One of my first true loves.

Opening up a need I didn't even know existed.

The need to feel it.

Smell it.

Be absorbed by it.

To be present.

With the bass thumping through my chest.

Boom

Boom

My First *True Love*

GRAHAM MacLENNAN

Graham lives with his beautiful wife on the beautiful Sunshine Coast of British Columbia. He divides his time between practising law and practising cooking. He also produces the podcast, *Cheftimony*, sharing stories from chefs and lawyers who love good food as much as he does.

Italian Food is Romance

I must have been inspired by the romantic comedies of the glorious 1980s because this love story begins in the library stacks, as many of them did in that era.

I was fifteen, finding my way through high school in the remote city of Thunder Bay. In with the cool kids I was not. I preferred books to parties and cooking to sports. But I liked the library. It was a place of quiet and discovery. And then it was more.

I met them in the cooking section in the library basement, mid-way down the stack, second shelf from the bottom. There they were, tucked away on a dog-eared page of a well-thumbed Italian cookbook. On those tomato-stained pages, I met gnocchi for the first time, and I've been in love ever since.

If you haven't met them, gnocchi are the pillowy morsels of potato that challenge chefs the world over. They can be made with as few as two ingredients: flour and potato. And when made that way (if the dough doesn't disintegrate in boiling water), they are a revelation. They taste more like potato than does potato. They offer the tiniest resistance to your bite and then dissolve, coating your tastebuds in flavour.

Gnocchi have been with me through bachelorhood and relationships, happy days and tragedy. I'm convinced they played a foundational role in my marriage. While dating, my wife-to-be and I prepared gnocchi together for a friend's New Year's Eve party. Many hours in the kitchen preparing one simple dish demonstrated the point in practice much better than I could in words: Cooking is really, really important to me.

If you like—and if you're brave—you can add egg to your gnocchi dough to help bind it. It will make your gnocchi easier to work with. It will also make the resulting morsels denser, depending on the amount of egg and the force of your kneading. That addition of egg will also expose you to derision from the potato-and-flour-and-that's-it crowd. Stand your ground. They're your gnocchi and you love them, so defend them.

But let's talk about "simple." Over time, I have learned that "simple" and "easy" are two different things. Easy is always easy. Simple is always simple. But it's rare for simple and easy to live happily together. Gnocchi are simple. They are also bloody difficult. Sometimes they refuse to stick together in doughy morsels. Sometimes they do stick, only to turn into starchy liquid in the pot. Staying in a happy relationship with gnocchi requires effort—rather a lot of effort. The good news is that the effort brings reward, and not only in the form of delicious food.

It turns out that effort and repetition are the twin solutions to the problem that plagues every relationship: advice. Have you noticed that everyone is an expert on *your* relationship? I've found that the same applies in the culinary world. Over the years, I have received countless pieces of advice for making the best gnocchi, much of it contradictory and all of it based on what worked for someone else, in their relationship with their recipe.

The key, I've found, is to keep at it, to keep practising, to keep trying. Some of the pieces of advice worked for me, but only after I'd tried them many times—only after I'd incorporated them into my own process. The secret is that there is no secret. There's no tip that's going to transform your gnocchi from acceptable to world class. There is only work and repetition.

So, if you want to love gnocchi as I do, put in the work. Repeat what made them happy the last time, let go of whatever isn't serving them. Try again and see how it goes. Sometimes your efforts won't work at all, and then you're best to give gnocchi a little time on their own. But come back to them. Take the time. Make the effort. You may find the most delicious thing you've ever known. And that's a love worth knowing.

ANONYMOUS

I wish the author of this song would have allowed me to use his name, but that is not to be. So I must content myself with singing this song once again in Tucson, Arizona, when I get together with his appreciative friends.

The Minnesota–Norwegian Fisherman's Anthem

(Sung to the tune of "Oh Tannenbomb"—misspelling intentional)
Oh Lutefisk, Oh Lutefisk, I dream at night of eating you!
You look so white; you shake just right;
too bad your smell is out of sight!
Yet I can't help but loving you.
I don't know why you taste like glue.
But as for me, I'll tell you this:
You are the best of all the fisk.

Oh Lutefisk, Oh Lutefisk, you make such lovely shingles,
And paving streets or papering walls,

You're also great as Pringles.
So many ways of using you,
X-Lax is not as good as you.
Yes Lutefisk, you're just like Torsk;
You make me proud to be a Norsk!

JASON THOMPSON

Jason lives in Niverville, Manitoba, where, he tells me, he parents proudly, golfs poorly, brokers insurance, and keeps his grass cut. Like Michelle Kube, Jason's first love was music—but a highly specific type of music.

The King

My earliest memories from the mid-1970s involve my fanatical love for the music of the legendary Elvis Presley. My dad would play Elvis Presley eight-tracks in our old yellow Pontiac on a cutting-edge, 8-track player, and we had a box of tapes on the floor of the car. This small, hard-covered, black box with faux-crocodile skin, red-velvet interior, and a silver handle held a dozen 8-track tapes. But only two mattered to me. One 8-track was blue, and the other was pink—and they both said ELVIS. I believe these were K-Tel's Elvis compilations because most of the songs were quite obscure, with only a handful of his best hits sprinkled into the mix. Some of my favourite Elvis songs early on were those that nobody else had ever heard. Nonetheless, I could not get enough of these pink and blue Elvis 8-tracks, and they'd often be used

My First *True Love*

as a bribe—played only if my sister and I would stop fighting in the backseat of that old yellow Pontiac. My dad would try to play Johnny Cash, Dolly Parton, or Hank Williams, but I wanted Elvis...ALL THE TIME, every time. I would grab that black, 8-track carrier case and immediately insist that he play the pink one...and then the blue...and then the pink one again. I always got my way.

I was five in 1977, which was a pivotal year in a couple of ways. The yellow Pontiac was sold in favour of some new family wheels. I cried and cried as Dad handed the keys to the young man standing in our driveway. I couldn't understand why we'd be parting with this perfectly good car. It made little sense. The sadness quickly subsided, however, when I joined my dad in picking up a shiny new white Monte Carlo in Steinbach—The Auto City. I was happy to learn that the new Monte had an 8-track tape player and that the black 8-track container with those two Elvis tapes would be joining us in the new car. It mattered only that our car could play those Elvis 8-tracks.

Sadness struck later that same year and in a bigger way. My dad announced that Elvis had died, and I cried, standing in that same driveway. (I suppose it was customary in 1977 to deliver bad news in the driveway.) Devastating. Lots of tears.

Eventually I got over the utter devastation of 1977. We had a cabin in the early 1980s, and every weekend included my playing the record in the big, orange album cover entitled *Elvis' Golden Records*. This official RCA album was not the watered-down K-tel variety. This album contained ALL the early Elvis hits, and I wore that sucker out during my weekend visits to the cabin.

My first-ever concert took place around 1980, when my mum took me to the Centennial Concert Hall in Winnipeg to see Elvis impersonators. An impersonator seemed like a rip-off of an idea, so I was less than excited at first, but it was actually quite good. Mum even managed for us to meet two of the impersonators, and I got two signed, black-and-white "Elvis" photos. One signed photo was of the traditional, black-leather-clad, 1950's Elvis. The other was a sequined, jump-suited, 1970's Fat Elvis. These impersonators were still dear to me, and the signed photos held a prominent place in my room for quite a while. I was eight around the time of that concert, and it was a good experience because, despite Elvis's death a few years earlier, I had retained my love for all things Elvis, and I was still young enough to go to a concert with my mother.

My love for Elvis's songs virtually disappeared in adolescence, as my musical taste morphed into late 1980's gangster rap, early 1990's grunge, and other far more aggressive sounds. Very un-Elvis music occupied my mixtapes. The fake-Elvis photos disappeared in favour of Run DMC, Nirvana, and Public Enemy posters. The black 8-track tape box was long gone, and the tapes had long been garbled up by the player. I had my own wheels now, and my sound system preferred something much, much, different. Elvis wasn't dead to me, but he was on life support. My love didn't survive my teens with the same fervour.

I'm no longer an Elvis fanatic. I've never been to Graceland, and I may never go. Elvis's music is not on my Spotify list. There are still flashes of my first love on certain occasions, however. Relatives did supply a surprise Elvis impersonator when Sue and I were married in 2000, and it was awesome. The entire wedding party danced to the jumpsuit 1970's version of Elvis. It was a cheesy surprise add-on to our otherwise elegant wedding and a definite highlight. Clearly my early fandemonium left an impression on people all those years later! And our daughter performed as Elvis in her Grade 5 talent show just a handful of years ago—complete with jumpsuit and the famous silver Elvis glasses. I loved that! She seemed quite natural somehow.

Every year around Christmas, I'll watch at least one Elvis concert—usually alone because it doesn't capture the interest of anyone else in the family. My favourites are *Aloha from Hawaii* from 1973 and *Elvis Unplugged* from 1968. The saddest videos are those last concerts in 1977, when a drugged-up, unhealthy, and obese Elvis slurs his way through his songs just months before his death by drug overdose. Fortunately, I have memories of the 8-track Elvis I knew and loved during those car rides in the old yellow Pontiac and the white Monte. I love those early memories that are some of the most vivid of my early childhood.

Come to think of it, perhaps a trip to Graceland is in order!

LORRAINE SPROXTON

Lorraine is a prairie girl, born in Winnipeg, Manitoba, where the Red and Assiniboine Rivers meet and eventually flow into Lake Winnipeg—or, as some people call it, "The Prairie Ocean." Her astrological sign is Pisces, which confirms for her that Lake Winnipeg was in her blood from the beginning.

Romancing the Lake

My maternal grandfather lived in the Town of Winnipeg Beach, where he was Magistrate, Sheriff, and Secretary of the Town Council. Even better, he had a cottage on Park Avenue, and from the first time I can remember, every summer was spent on the beach at The Lake. And during the spring flood of 1950 in Winnipeg, we spent a few weeks at Grandpa's house. In fact, I recall languishing on his couch after receiving the tuberculosis vaccine via a 10-foot needle. (I'm sure it was that long.) Grandpa had a Victrola—His Master's Voice—gramophone, and he would play my favourite record, "Ghost Riders in the Sky." But I digress....

My dad was a pharmacist—druggists, as they were called back then—and he was unable to come to The Lake as frequently as the rest of the family or stay as long as we could. So my mother, my older sister, and I would usually take the steam train from Union Station in Winnipeg to The Lake.

As I write this, I recall with great nostalgia the huge, noisy, steel engine; the constant but lulling chugga-chugga of the train as it pulled us toward our destination; and stories about the moonlight trains that brought young men and women to The Lake for weekend fun—dancing at the huge dance hall, walking on the pier and on the boardwalk. Every word filled my young mind with thoughts of endless romance that were forever associated with The Lake.

After what seemed like hours, my beckoning lake suddenly appeared out of the train window, and I can still feel the butterflies in my stomach at that sight, as I anticipated the fun and excitement of summer days. Soon those carefree days would begin, along with the many visits from cousins, aunts, uncles, and friends.

The train also carried important letters from The Lake to Winnipeg, and they would arrive at their destination in only one or two days. Important mail, like the letter I sent to my dad, giving him specific instructions about which doll I needed him to bring when he came to Winnipeg Beach: "Not the big doll, but the doll with the napkins (a drawing of 2 rectangles) and bring the napkins too." I ended the letter with, "I have to go now because we are going to the sand."

All was well with my world. The train would carry my letter to my dad, the doll would arrive with him, and the sand and The Lake would all be in place.

The inner eyes of childhood memories can see us fetching pails of water from the hand pump on the street beside our cottage; the iceman delivering ice for the icebox that served as our refrigerator; the "honey wagon" emptying the outhouse; the family eating many meals of that Lake Winnipeg delicacy, fresh-caught pickerel; kids learning to ride bikes, playing cards and board games, playing hide and seek in the large yard, waving at the engineer and passengers at the nearby train crossing, playing on the train tracks with older siblings, and seeking revenge during our many games of croquet.

We had to walk to the beach from the cottage. The adults would pack lunches, towels, sun lotion, sun hats, bathing caps, sand pails, and shovels; our well-patched, blow-up flotation whale; and the well-patched, blow-up beach ball. Off we would go to spend the day on the beach, splashing in the water, building sandcastles and forts, collecting shells and wishing hard that one day there would be a pearl hiding in one of those shells, or collecting the unique stones that had washed up from the depths and breadth of ancient Lake Agassiz. Sometimes we would find a dead fish that had come upon the shore—always a great source of reluctant fascination.

The romantic boardwalk remained along the beachfront at that time, and it was a wonderful treat when we were allowed to board the merry-go-round, "win" prizes at the duck pond, or ride the ponies. There was a huge and intimidating wooden roller coaster that I was too young to ride—and if the truth be known, I think it was a relief. There were the best French fries ever made (we called them "chips") and the finely spun sugar that was cotton candy. Even though the majestic dance pavilion was no longer operating, everything was magical to me and supported my romantic imagination.

The beach and lake—My Lake—were never the same. The hard-to-predict winds control the various water movements, so that the radio broadcasts included a marine forecast for the fishers and various crafts. I loved its ever-changing fancy, making it an exciting surprise each day. I have often told people that I have always loved being in, on, or near My Lake. It is always beckoning me to come to it. It's musical: music when the water gently laps at the shore, a fuller musical energy when there are whitecaps on the water, and a thrilling climactic cacophony of sound when the huge waves smack the shore with a resounding "Boom." Sitting by my quiet lake, I enjoy watching a large variety of water birds. But the ones I love best are the pelicans. When they ride on top of The Lake, they indeed look like aristocratic senators—always watching for and looking after the best interests of My Lake.

The death of my grandfather concluded my childhood relationship with My Lake; I was fortunate as an adult, however, to return and incorporate my own family into the world of Lake Winnipeg. But that is another story for another time.

As the reader might already have guessed, no matter what, my first love will never end.

MARJORIE ANDERSON

Life has taken Marjorie through travels, family making, studies in English literature, and careers in teaching and editing. She currently lives in Winnipeg with her husband, Gary, and revels in their children (four), grandchildren (nine), and great-grandchildren (two). Now that her first true love is back occasionally, they take off at a more sedate pace, for places where the philosophic mind can contemplate Wordsworth's "splendor in the grass and glory in the flower." New destinations that suit the reuniting of old flames.

Sojo on My Mind

He first appeared to me on a sweltering day in August 1956, near my childhood home on the shores of Netley-Libau Marsh. There I was, stretched out on a stubble field gazing up at clouds scudding by, when one of them took the shape of a horse. Not an ordinary horse, but a magnificent white stallion in full gallop with a silky mane streaming over his arched neck. In an instant, I was on his back with the wind in my hair, bare legs pressed against his flanks, my body insubstantial, as if reduced to a mere rush of heartbeats. The rhythmic call of shore birds followed us as we streaked, comet-like, across the sky. The vision lasted seconds, a minute at most. Then the wind shifted, and what had been my horse broke up and sailed off as wisps of ordinary cloud. I was suddenly back in my tethered body, lying in a hay field where I had snatched a break from the numbing chore of herding cows home for milking time.

The elation from that experience stayed with me like a pulse of light in the bleakness of my pre-teen rural existence. Sojo—that's what I named him—became etched into my twelve-year-old brain; I could access him anytime by simply closing my eyes and feeling his surging power beneath me. In a flash, the isolation and poverty of my life would fall away, and my mother's singing call from the barn, "Cow time, Marjorie," would miraculously mute as Sojo and I galloped off. Sometimes there'd be no destination; we'd simply join the play of light and movement in the open sky. At other times, we'd arrive at some future shining place where I *knew*

I was destined to be—bowing to applause beside my piano on a concert stage in Europe; singing with my soaring Patsy-Cline voice at the Grand Ole Opry in Nashville; or, most often, in a garret in a vine-covered brick building in England, writing novels or having tea with Agatha Christie.

But imaginary first loves have a way of dissipating, especially when they smack up against reality. In Grade 11, I had a boyfriend, a sweet, ardent farm boy who rode with me on the school bus. As a birthday treat that May, he arranged for us to go horseback riding at a local farm. I had never actually been on the back of a horse until then. We did own two lanky draft horses, Bony and Charlie, who often stood in the shade outside my bedroom window, snorting, stomping, and swatting flies with their tails. (Clearly a separate species from Sojo.) It had never occurred to me to get on their backs. But on that spring day, I did mount an actual living, breathing creature, only to discover, horrified, that its back was as high as a barn roof and as wide and hard as a barrel. My body remembered instantly that I was terrified of heights. My legs strained and clutched at its belly; my hands gripped the reins like a drowning person with a life raft. The owner of the horse, not noticing my body language, may have gently slapped its flanks to get it trotting, but to me she had whipped it into a frenzied gallop that ended with my screaming to get off and my companion burning with embarrassment.

A few things were marred that day—my pride, for one, along with the unwavering admiration of my boyfriend. But most dramatically, my imagined escapes with Sojo. I could *not* project myself onto the back of a horse again. Height and terror had replaced freedom and ecstasy. The clouds over my farmyard stayed in their usual formations and my stallion didn't emerge again when I closed my eyes, not there and not in the years following when I migrated to the city for college, work, and, eventually, marriage and family.

But another thing about first loves—the visceral memory of them tends to resurface in later years. I am now in my seventies and find that, on occasion, Sojo is on my mind again. Sometimes, when my knees creak and throb and I double-step every stair I walk down, when I can't bend to do this anymore or leap to catch that, an old familiar feeling of confinement returns. That's when Sojo reappears, still splendid, still with glistening flanks throbbing beneath my bare skin. And then we're off, hair and mane magically together like strands of silk flowing behind us as we gallop away, just away, from the pull of reality.

GAYLEEN HUTCHINGS

Gayleen has worked in a pharmacy, a public utility, the public school system, and a university. She and her husband, Brian, are now enjoying retirement.

My Favourite Dress

I grew up in a dysfunctional home. My father was an alcoholic for thirteen years of my life. It was not an easy or happy time. We were poor, and money was tight, to say the least. At Christmas we usually received a Christmas orange, some Christmas candies, and a small gift from our parents. We also got a hamper from our church, and we were grateful to receive it. My father eventually hit rock bottom, admitted that he had a drinking problem, and joined AA. He did quit drinking, but it was emotionally hard on all of us. It was like walking on eggshells, as one never knew what would set him off.

And then one year, when times were a bit better, I received a new dress for Christmas from my parents—an orange Dan River gingham dress. I can still picture it today. It had short sleeves, a collar, buttons down the front to the waist, a gathered skirt, and a belt. I loved that dress. I felt good when I wore it, and I thought I looked pretty good in it too. My parents must have saved for some time to purchase gifts for all four of us kids.

I loved that dress then, and I love the memory of it now. It's a good memory. I have a much better life today, but I never forget where I came from. And I'll never forget my first true love.

ANN MacDONALD

Ann was born in a small Scottish town on August 15, 1945—on the last day of World War II. She immigrated to Canada in 1964 and lived for many years in Kamloops and Vancouver, British Columbia. She now resides in Edmonton, Alberta. Her career has centred around the law: the RCMP, corporate lawyers, family lawyers, and prosecution services; she has also served as the manager of a small law firm. Ann has two sons, two granddaughters, and five grandsons. Her many interests include needlework and Scottish country dancing.

Oh-h-h-h-h Canada!!

It's a cold, bleak, Scottish day, and I'm sitting on the top level of a double-decker bus taking me to work. Just then another jet arrives at Prestwick Airport, and as its landing path goes across the main road, all traffic comes to a stop. I watch this huge monster landing with a thump and then fishtailing before stopping. I was scheduled to depart on such an aircraft in two weeks to join my boyfriend in Canada, but at that moment, I got cold feet and decided not to make the trip.

Luckily, I plucked up enough courage and eventually did depart for Canada, arriving in Kamloops, British Columbia on March 23, 1964. On the drive from Vancouver Airport to Kamloops, we passed through the spectacular scenery of the Fraser Canyon, like nothing I had ever seen in Scotland.

This place, Canada, blew me away, and I fell in love with it immediately. Coming from a small village in Scotland, where class distinction and religion were very prevalent, I marvelled at how everyone seemed to be treated equally. There were no row houses, all the streets were clean, and people were so friendly. I was able to get a job within a week of my arrival and was gainfully employed until I retired over fifty years later.

There was a moment, nine months after arriving in Canada, when things did not seem to be working too well with my boyfriend, and I thought about going back home. I didn't want to do that because I had already come to love this country, so I decided to tough it out and stay. It is a decision for which I will always be thankful.

I remember one trip I took to Scotland with my two young sons, and upon arriving in Canada and deplaning in Kamloops, I literally got down on my hands and knees and kissed the tarmac. That's how much I had missed it.

Scotland is a beautiful country, with wonderful vistas and beaches, and I am glad that I was born there. But Canada has such diverse regions, from the Prairies to the Rocky Mountains to the East Coast, with so many wonderful things to see. I have been to many countries and would consider Vancouver the most beautiful city in the world.

I was born in Scotland, but I truly consider myself a proud Canadian and believe that Canada is the best country in the world to live. I do consider it my first true love.

KATRINA ANDERSON (aka FONTANA SWING)

Born a proud prairie girl, Katrina now lives in the Blue Mountains in Ontario. She spends much of her time running a virtual music school, painting, drawing, writing, and of course, playing her dream piano, a classic Yamaha C3 Grand…in bare feet.

Dear Piano, I Love You

Dear Miss Neufeld,

1969 brown "lady shoes," pumping up and down on silver pedals that grow out of the piano. You said it was okay for me to move my napping mat right up close to those pedals. Right up close to your lady shoes, pumping away. Even better, you let me press my kindergarten ear against the shaky wooden belly of the piano while your sleepy lullabies filled the classroom air. None of the other kids even wanted a turn napping so close to you, to the piano. Maybe they asked. Maybe you said, "No, no, that spot is for Kat. She needs to sleep there." I did need that spot.

My First *True Love*

My spot.
Your shoes.
Our duet.

My parents bought me a piano that same first year of school.

My parents bought me that very piano, your piano, the piano I fell in love with at naptime.

Our piano.
Our pedals.

This very same piano still lives in my parents' home. And though I now own six pianos, two of them in a new home, in a new city, playing new songs, it is *our* piano that I loved first.

It's true.
It was the first.
Love.

Love Knows No Bounds

And Where Can Love Be Found?

> Love says,
> "Open your arms and fly with me."
>
> *- Emmanuel's Book II: The Choice for Love*

Here are three stories that exemplify for me the breadth and the depth of love. There's a story about self-love; a story about the many faces of love; and a story of the search for love and the realization that love can arrive a second time, unexpectedly and powerfully.

LIANE FAULDER

An award-winning journalist and columnist for *Postmedia's* "Senior Living" series, Liane is the author of *The Long Walk Home: Paul Franklin's*

Journey from Afghanistan. The 2007 book chronicles the inspiring recovery of an Edmonton soldier who lost both legs in a suicide bombing and was the inspiration for Liane's play, *WALK*, which won the 2015 Alberta Playwright's Network Discovery prize. *WALK* debuted before packed houses at the 2018 Edmonton International Fringe Festival.

Later in life, Liane met her true love, Terry Daniel. She is grateful every day for that and for the blessing of two boys, now grown men, who can always make her laugh.

My Own. My Jane.

My first love could be described only as plain. Thin and sallow, with a penchant for dressing in black, she had no taste for adornments. Because she was cautious in relationships, people assumed she was haughty. When she was able to attract a lover by virtue of her intellect, her peers were surprised; they had already dismissed her, blindly accepting that pretty trumped a talent for watercolours any day of the week.

Her name? It was Jane. Jane Eyre.

My mother, little knowing the effect Jane would have on me, gave me a hardcover edition of the Charlotte Bronte classic for Christmas the year I turned twelve. The steadfast governess has stayed close to my heart ever since. I read the book a dozen times, back to back, the first year I owned it, thereafter returning for inspiration throughout my teens when my pimples were really bad, or my boyfriend had broken up with me—again.

Those trials were meaningless next to Jane's.

Raised in an orphanage known mostly for chilblains, Jane once awoke to find her best friend dead beside her in bed. Even as an adult, she was forced to stumble through a wide glen, in the rain, for three days, without so much as a teacake for sustenance. A mad woman tried to set her on fire. I couldn't match Jane for hardship (though I did have to babysit my brothers for an extremely low wage). But there was something we had in common, and this is why I both loved her deeply and saw her as a mentor.

Jane was overlooked by those around her. But she never underestimated herself. Despite repeated messages to the contrary, she saw value in her own humble gifts.

Oh, and there were times when it might have seemed prudent to take whatever dirt was dished her way because, after all, it was the nineteenth century and prospects for homely orphans were limited. When her beloved, Mr. Rochester, proposed that he and Jane live together on the Continent, after it was revealed that he was trapped in a loveless marriage, Jane refused.

Tucked under my chenille bedspread, reading late into the night (wearing a pair of my mother's cotton dress gloves on my hands because, of course, I had eczema), I howled in agony. "Jane," I explained, hoping she would see reason, "it's France. Nobody would even know."

When the rector of that damp glen wanted her to be his wife so he would have company on an upcoming mission to Africa, once again, she demurred.

"Okay, he's a bit of a cold fish," I acknowledged, my desperation growing, "but he's handsome. And you love his sisters. Don't forget, you're almost twenty. Your best years are behind you."

Jane thought she could do better. And in the end, she did.

I would like to say that, with Jane's support, I went on to make a lifetime's worth of great choices for myself, secure in the knowledge that I had value. But this was not always the case, and there was a regrettable series of men who did not throw down their coats so I could avoid a puddle.

"That's okay," I said to reassure them, "I've got other shoes."

The great thing about a role model like Jane, however, is that she never leaves you. One day, I woke up and decided that, like Jane, I'd be happier living in a small but well-organized cottage, with only my needlepoint for company. As Jane knew, that was enough. It is more than enough. But here's something interesting. Once I had made that decision, just like in a novel, my beloved appeared.

Jane, in her quiet way, was pleased.

Happily-ever-after, though, is never really the end of the story. Life continues to demand that we believe in ourselves enough to persevere, and not just in love. Sometimes, when I imagine I'm not up for the challenges coming my way and begin to doubt my own instincts, I reach into my closet in search of a black dress. Fixing a modest brooch to my bosom, I head into the world, and there she is, with me again. My own, my dearest, my Jane.

EMILY A. BRYANT

Emily was awarded the Order of Prince Edward Island in 2012 for her contribution to nursing, mental health, and her community. And although she didn't mention it when I asked her for a bio sketch, she's a fine singer, who has performed for many years in church choirs and in the gospel group, Jericho Road. "Being named after a grandmother and a great-grandmother," Emily contends, "set me up for close, life-long family ties."

And Where Can Love Be Found?

The Many Faces of Love

Having dated my husband for five years and having been married to him for fifty-eight years makes it difficult for me to look beyond the relationship I share with him. Yet at the end of my time on this earth, I want my life to include but not be confined to the meaningful relationship I share with my husband and my immediate family. I love them so much that I hurt when they hurt and rejoice when they triumph. I have loved my family and my life—with all the hills and valleys.

But I have cared deeply about many things—cared passionately even. I've talked about my passions more than most people wanted to hear. I've even written an autobiography about my life and my nursing career. How I loved my work in mental health! I experienced Eureka moments when a patient recovered from a serious depression or when I advocated for and saw the benefits of an innovative approach to mental-health services. I was thrilled when I taught principles of empathy and watched my students grasp those principles and became therapeutic communicators. I loved those moments of making a difference.

I still long to make a difference in mental health, although, as a retiree, I am no longer on the front lines. I continue to write letters advocating improved mental-health services. I speak up when I hear of policies with the potential to negate steps that were designed to reduce struggles for people with mental-health disorders. In many ways, then, my nursing career, spanning more than forty years, was and continues to be my first true work love.

I am and always have been smitten with gardening. As a child, I remember planting a vegetable garden and a flower garden with my grandfather and my parents, and I remember my excitement when the seeds began to grow. I even like weeding now, although I probably didn't always think that way. I find working in our warm, red Prince Edward

Island soil to be peaceful and soothing. So, gardening would be my first true hobby love.

Gardening leads me to think about cooking and food. Sometimes I feel that I may have been born in the wrong century, for food preservation is not really needed now. It is, in fact, a dying art. It could be argued that it's easy to buy pickles tastier than I can make and probably even more cheaply. But there's the satisfaction of canning or creating a meal that leads me to call the preserving and serving of food a love interest.

Oh, how lucky I was to be born on Prince Edward Island and to live here my entire life. This little Canadian province has beautiful scenery all seasons of the year. The fields are green and lush in spring and summer. The soil is a soft red and rich and fertile. Being on an island, we can see beautiful water—rivers and gulfs—from many directions. We seldom have winter snowstorms that disrupt our lives; nor do we undergo unbearably, dangerously hot summer days. This island has rarely experienced hurricanes, tornados, or other natural disasters. We enjoy stunning sunrises and sunsets. No wonder thousands of tourists love to visit this "gentle island" every year. It offers so much! It has offered me joy all my life. I have had limited exposure to other parts of the world. I'm like the Islander in the joke about the visitor who said that he was from a city of several million—to which the Islander responded, "What a pity. So many people away from everything here." I would have to say that Prince Edward Island, my home, is another of my first true loves.

At the risk of sounding completely Pollyanna, I want to finish my list of first true loves to include my family—my family of origin and my current family, including my extended family—my wonderful parents and siblings; my wonderful aunts, uncles, and cousins. With cousins, I share a grandfather on both my mother's and father's side. And they all agree with me: Grandfathers give us treasured memories. I never knew a grandmother, as they had both died before I was born, but my paternal grandfather lived with us, and he made up for this loss. My cousins were my classmates at school, my workmates with farm chores, and my playmates when work was done. No wonder they have a special place in my heart. At this time, in my senior years, with all our parents gone, I remain close to my cousins—good people I would love even if we were not kin.

My family of origin is my first true love—a foundation that taught me to value family and to become a decent wife and a not-too-shabby mother, a foundation that leaves me with lots of love left over for our grandchildren. My family will be an ongoing true love to my final days. And because my first true love of family blends with my present family, my love story never ends.

LILLY JULIA SCHUBERT WALKER-KITTSLEY

From North Dakota to Manitoba, from Newfoundland to New York, Lilly's life reflects her passions for psychology, people, and play.

The Search for True Love

What is love? My search for this elusive feeling began in Grade 7. Perhaps love is the butterflies in my stomach caused by my dreamy-eyed crush on the oh-so-handsome football coach and my science teacher; or my first tentative kiss with the tall, blond, bashful boy whose ring I wore around my neck for a week, signifying our status of "going steady." Maybe it's when my heart skipped a beat each time the football captain noticed me in the school hallway or the excitement of wearing his letter jacket to a football game during the one week he had broken up with his long-time girlfriend. Fleeting moments of powerful positive emotions, which contrasted with the usual feelings of awkwardness, gloomy insecurity, and unattractiveness that permeated my consciousness. During my teen years, when my friends had dates for dances and boyfriends who took them to movies, I was home-bound, crying myself to sleep and doubting I would ever find that illusory, mysterious thing called love.

My search continued into the questioning college years, when lofty life questions filled night-time discussions, and the pursuit of meaning and purpose framed my thoughts, actions, and conversations. Dating, though confusing and disappointing, provided clues to what love was and was not.

The unexpected experience of meeting for the first time someone who appreciated qualities in me I did not see in myself and opened me to a process of self-discovery was electrifying. Perhaps love is being fully seen. He shared with me the wonder of the intellectual world of ideas, challenged me, and valued my academic abilities and cognitive capabilities. He saw more than I could see, and his attention and adulation made me feel beautiful. Perhaps love is feeling cherished. Through this relationship, I discovered that feeling of love that opens us to others and ourselves. As this relationship evolved and matured, there were times of joyful togetherness interspersed with the heartache of separation and the despair of disengagement. Sometimes love hurts.

The search continued. Amidst the academic pressures of graduate school came the gentle embrace and supportive quiet touch of a future life partner who would be beside me through forty years of life's changes and challenges, joys and sorrows, victories and defeats. Intelligent and introverted, serious and studious, analytical and wise, he was someone

And Where Can Love Be Found?

who shared my passion for psychology and nurtured my professional aspirations. Yet he was my opposite; he completed me. Perhaps love is finding wholeness through connection. He awakened my soul, opened me to possibilities, ignited my passions, planted fire in my heart, and promised to love me forever. He put me first, brought out the best in me, encouraged, uplifted, supported, and sacrificed. He was my first true love, who shared professional success, the comfortable rhythms of ordinary days, the discoveries that life brings, and the joys of parenthood.

As thunder roared and lightning flashed throughout the Manitoba skies on July 6, 1975, I experienced the awe-inspiring, primal, profoundly powerful love that the birth of a child brings. From the first moment of holding this tiny, fragile son in my arms, I felt the transformative presence of the deep emotional bond between us. This is an instinctive love that nurtures and anticipates, provides and plays, believes and hopes, teaches and remembers. This is a love that creates. This is a love that changed us both.

Time teaches, love evolves; I learned that love is a soulmate who consistently cares, understands me like no other, loves me unconditionally, is an equalitarian life partner, and is there for me no matter what. This is a love of growing side by side with tangled roots and reaching branches. It has taught me that being loved brings strength, and that loving someone takes courage.

Love bears all things. The unexpected diagnosis of my true love's untreatable colon cancer changed our lives. The future uncertain, all we had was today. Simple daily activities mattered. Experiencing the emotional roller coaster and unpredictability of cancer treatment, we found strength in leaning on one another. Conversations changed. Taboo topics were discussed. Each day we grew closer to one another. Time together was precious.

In the intimacy of our final days together, as death wrenched him from my arms, I discovered the agony of loss and the bravery needed to let go. Through days together that defined our life story, I discerned that love involves seeking, sharing, sustaining, sacrificing, and surviving.

Aging brings perspective to this search…partners die, children leave home to commence their own lives, and grandchildren bring hugs and hope. Remembering love-filled moments brings joy. Appreciating the myriad ways that love has enriched and coloured my days brings closure to the search.

The serendipity of finding love again was extraordinarily wonderful. Meeting someone who found beauty in a face full of the lines of smiles experienced and tears shed was exciting. His pursuit ignited passions that hid a hungry heart. He made me laugh, brought joy to each day, and encouraged me to play. Here was a man who treasured me and created a long list of the reasons he loved me. Being together made the ordinary magical. In opening me to the vulnerability and ecstasy that is love shared, I discovered again the promise and adventure that is love. Together we discovered that age does not protect one from love, but love protects one from aging.

* * *

The discovery I made through this life-long search is that love is an encounter with another that ignites our spirits, changes our worldviews, creates our identities, and brings meaning and purpose to our days.

Love is a life-transforming gift.

Acknowledgements

Foremost in the long list of people to whom I am eternally grateful are the seventy-eight storytellers who provided me—and therefore you—with their stories. They underwent edits, provided bio sketches, and waited patiently for this book to be released. Their names all appear twice: once in the Table of Contents and once in their stories, so here I will merely say, "Thank you. Thank you. Thank you."

Thank you to Dale and Billy and Dempsey and Rae, who inspired this book.

Thank you to the generous people who provided me with feedback on myriad issues: Dennis Anderson, Marjorie Anderson, Maureen Arnason, Carol Dahlstrom, Gary Martin, Pat Sanders, Tanya Speight, and Bill Valgardson. I shudder to think of the errors that would have slipped by without your keen eyes.

Thank you, Rachelle Painchaud-Nash for your creative ideas; your primary characteristic, after competence, must be patience.

And thank you, the wonderfully helpful and competent people at Friesen: Adam, the Editor; Joanna Vieira, the Designer; and Brittany Peters and Madison Shymberg, the Publishing Specialists.

Printed in Canada